BRIT. LIT.
Volume 1

OLD ENGLISH

Versification by
DOUGLAS WILSON

OLD ENGLISH

Selected and Edited by
REBEKAH MERKLE

LOGOS PRESS
MOSCOW • IDAHO

Published by Logos Press
P.O. Box 8729, Moscow, ID 83843
800.488.2034 | www.logospressonline.com

Rebekah Merkle, ed., *Brit Lit, Vol. 1: Old English*
Copyright © 2015 by Rebekah Merkle.
Beowulf translation and essays copyright © 2013 by Douglas Wilson. Used by permission.

Cover and interior design by Rebekah Merkle.
Printed in the United States of America.

All rights reserved. No part of this publication may be reproduced, stored in a retrieval system, or transmitted in any form by any means, electronic, mechanical, photocopy, recording, or otherwise, without prior permission of the author, except as provided by USA copyright law.

Library of Congress Cataloging-in-Publication Data is forthcoming.

BEOWULF

Versification by DOUGLAS WILSON

CONTENTS:

Introduction	13
Beowulf	21
Beowulf: The UnChrist	175
Chiastic Structure in *Beowulf*	193
Answer Key	201

READING SCHEDULE

This Old English segment should take you a grand total of fifteen days, including the test. Here's the official schedule:

DAY 1:	Reading 1 in this volume	13
DAY 2:	Reading 2 in this volume	21
	The Hobbit: Chapter 1	
	Poetry Workbook: Lesson 1	
DAY 3:	Reading 3 in this volume	37
	The Hobbit: Chapters 2-3	
	Poetry Workbook: Lesson 2	
DAY 4:	Reading 4 in this volume	49
	The Hobbit: Chapter 4	
	Poetry Workbook: Lesson 3	
DAY 5:	Reading 5 in this volume	59
	The Hobbit: Chapter 5	
	Poetry Workbook: Lesson 4	
DAY 6:	Reading 6 in this volume	73
	The Hobbit: Chapter 6	
	Poetry Workbook: Lesson 5	
DAY 7:	Reading 7 in this volume	87
	The Hobbit: Chapter 7	
	Poetry Workbook: Lesson 6	
DAY 8:	Reading 8 in this volume	101
	The Hobbit: Chapter 8	
	Poetry Workbook: Lesson 7	
DAY 9:	Reading 9 in this volume	113
	The Hobbit: Chapters 9-10	
	Poetry Workbook: Lesson 8	

Day 10:	Reading 10 in this volume *The Hobbit:* Chapters 11-12 *Poetry Workbook:* Lesson 9	125
Day 11:	Reading 11 in this volume *The Hobbit:* Chapters 13-14 *Poetry Workbook*: Lesson 10	137
Day 12:	Reading 12 in this volume *The Hobbit*: Chapters 15-17 *Poetry Workbook*: Lesson 11	147
Day 13:	Reading 13 in this volume *The Hobbit:* Chapters 18-19 *Poetry Workbook*: Lesson 12	161
Day 14:	Review all of your questions in this book. Review all poetic terminology from *Poetry Workbook*.	
Day 15:	Take test	

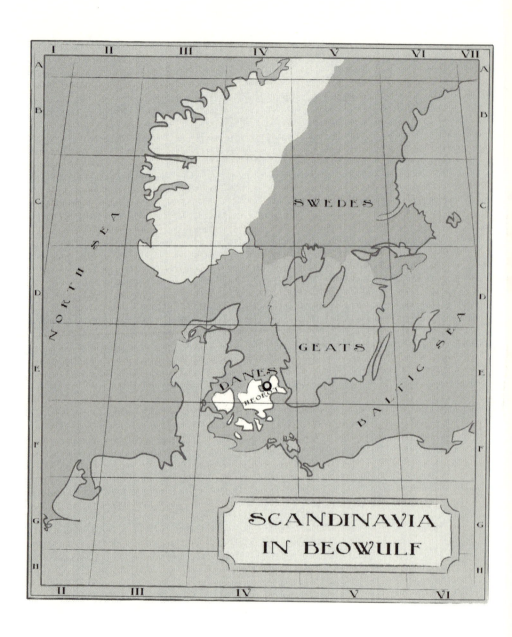

What's All This Then?

So you're about to launch a year long campaign into the literature and lore of Merry Old England. To be perfectly honest, I think it'll be a lot of fun, and we've tried to make this as user-friendly as possible. Here's how it works.

Every book is broken down into daily readings, and if you stick with reading your allotted portion every day then everything will be splendid. At the end of each day's reading you will find some questions. They're designed to make you think a bit, and may possibly require you to stretch your brain in uncomfortable ways. Answer them as best you can (in a notebook of some sort, ideally) and then once you've done so, compare your answers with the answers in the back of the book. Hang on to those answers. You'll need them to study for tests.

On most days, after you've gotten your head around those answers, you will turn to your *Poetry Workbook* and do the designated daily lesson. (Check the official schedule which will tell you which days you need to do this.) Then you're done for the day, and the only thing left for you to do is breathlessly count the minutes until you get to do it again upon the morrow.

This volume, as you may or may not have noticed, is the Old English portion of the series, and you are going to be reading the Anglo-Saxon poem *Beowulf* alongside J. R. R. Tolkien's *The Hobbit*. "For what possible reason?" I can hear you asking yourself. I'm so glad you brought this up. The reason you'll be reading these two books in tandem is this. Tolkien was not merely an author of fantasy adventure novels. That was just his hobby. The way he actually made his living was as a professor of Anglo-Saxon at Oxford University. This of course means that he was one of the top experts in the world on Anglo-Saxon literature, and his deep love of the subject very heavily influenced his own writings. So as you read *The Hobbit*, you should be paying attention to all the little details along the way where you can see that Tolkien is using the *Beowulf* story to add color, texture, or plot points to his own story. Try to resist the urge to barrel ahead and read the entire *Hobbit* in one gulp before you even finish the first chunk of *Beowulf*. Reading it at the same time is actually a really interesting experiment, so do your best to give it a whirl. And if you've read *The Hobbit* thirty-six times already . . . well, read it again.

A quick note on the *Poetry Workbook*. I'll just go ahead and level with you right now. You're going to write a lot of poetry this year and you're going to memorize a lot of poetry. If that gives you a fit of the vapors, go ahead and breath into a paper bag and then come back. The good news is, I'm sure you'll be awesome at it.

First Things First

Before we go galloping off into the wild world of Beowulf, there are a few things to get sorted out first. For instance, what do we mean by Anglo-Saxon? Who is Beowulf and why does he matter? If this is British Lit, why are we reading a story set in Scandinavia? Let's just get a few of those details ironed out before proceeding, shall we?

First, there's this whole question of what "Anglo-Saxon" means. If you grew up on Robin Hood, then you probably know about the tension between the Saxons and Normans. And if you're really hot on your European history then you'll know all about the Battle of Hastings and the Norman Invasion in 1066. But in order to understand who the Saxons were and how they ended up in England in the first place, you'll have to rewind for a moment to quite a bit earlier in the story.

Julius Caesar and his Roman troops made it to Britain in 55 BC as he was first expanding and establishing the Roman Empire. The natives of Britain at the time were a Celtic people known as Britons. After a number of invasions, the Romans had fairly effectively conquered the Britons and gradually civilized a goodish chunk of the island. Some of the natives remained unruly, and the Roman solution was basically to shove them out to the edges and keep them there. The center of the island, though, they settled and civilized.

Many of the Britons became Romanized and adapted themselves to the new way of life, and as the gospel was first being spread throughout the empire, it found its way to Britain as well. But right around the 400 AD mark, as I'm sure you know, the Roman Empire was beginning to get shaky. They began pulling the troops home from all the far-flung corners of the empire to attend to their problems at home, and the troops occupying Britain just basically up and left. This left all of those Romanized Britons in a terrible predicament. They had been protected by the Roman troops for centuries, but had never been taught how to defend or rule themselves. With their Roman protectors out of the picture, they were essentially sitting ducks. All the hostile (and untamable) tribes from the edges and corners of the island seized the moment and began making their way back in. The civilized Britons in the center desperately wrote to Rome for help but after a couple spurts of assistance, Rome officially cut all ties and told them they were on their own.

Meanwhile, across the North Sea, Scandinavia was full up with marauding Norsemen of the Viking variety. The Britons needed help defending themselves, and since Rome refused to give it, they hired themselves some Scandinavian mercenaries. Now you can see the obvious problem with this plan, and I can see the obvious problem with this plan, but the Britons were desperate. Of course the inevitable occurred. The mercenaries noticed what a lovely island Britain was, and how badly defended it was. They decided to go ahead and take it over themselves. There were three tribes in particular who targeted the helpless Britain: the Angles, the Saxons, and the Jutes. They were pagans who made their living by pirating, and were just the kind of people who would double-cross the defenseless people whom they had promised to help. They launched a flood of invasions, and eventually they took over Britain. (King Arthur, as you'll learn later, was a king of the Britons during this particular crisis who attempted to fight off these tribes and very nearly succeeded.)

Once the Angles, the Saxons, and the Jutes had settled in to Britain and began to get comfortable, they were harder to identify as three distinct tribes and they simply became known as Anglo-Saxons, or Saxons for short. (No one remembers the poor Jutes.) Incidentally, the name "England" is derived from this period of history. "Angle-land" eventually became "England," but the name "Britain" is a holdover from the earlier period when the Britons held it. Now we tend to use the names almost interchangeably, which is somewhat ironic given that the Britons and the Saxons were bitter and bloody enemies for centuries.

As the Saxons settled the country, they obviously were bringing with them the language, customs, and culture of their homeland. You should imagine England at this moment as being quite a linguistic hodgepodge of Celtic, and Latin, and the new Saxon language. And the culture itself was a muddle of Celtic paganism, Roman paganism, Saxon paganism, and Christianity. Needless to say, it was a rocky time.

After the Saxons had conquered England and gotten comfortable, they became Christians. Not all of a sudden, obviously, but it did eventually happen. Meanwhile, they were still telling the old heroic stories of their pagan homeland. It was in this context that an unknown Saxon poet put pen to paper and gave us *Beowulf*.

The only surviving manuscript is ambiguously dated as having been written between the eighth and the eleventh centuries. (Tolkien, incidentally, believed it to have been written in the eighth century.) The story itself, however, is set in the early sixth century. In essence, what we have with *Beowulf* is a poet who is living in England telling us the story of something that had happened much earlier, back in the motherland. Whether or not the poet composed the poem from scratch, or was merely writing down a previously existing poem which had been orally preserved is unknown.

The Poem

There are many questions surrounding *Beowulf*, the most obvious of which is, "Is it true?" As you read it, you'll notice things that couldn't possibly have happened, and you may then be tempted to write the whole thing off as impossible. However, although Beowulf himself is not mentioned in any other historical accounts that we possess, other characters are known to be actual figures in history, which is how we can date the events of the poem as having occurred in the early sixth century.

As Christians, how do we deal with the "fantastical" elements of stories like this one? Dragons? Monsters? Really? We're enlightened twenty-first century moderns, and we know better than to believe in those kinds of silly things, right? But sometimes we need to take a quick look around us and notice all the things that we do actually believe. Things that turn up at odd moments in the Old Testament: giants, dragons, pillars of salt, fallen angels, fiery chariots. Turns out we believe in lots of stuff that make enlightened twenty-first century moderns snicker. But if we do actually believe Scripture, and if we do actually think those things really happened, then the conclusion we must inevitably come to is that the world is a much crazier place than twenty-first century moderns like to think. So what do we do with stories like this one then? Do we decide that crazy things happened in Canaan but nowhere else?

There are several things to keep in mind. On the one hand, we can't write off these kinds of stories the way an atheistic evolutionist materialist would. But on the other hand, we need to remember is that we believe the events of Scripture actually happened because we know that Scripture is inspired by God, and we don't actually think anything of the kind about *Beowulf*. Just because the world is a crazy place doesn't mean that every crazy story is true.

So as you read, try and keep those two things in mind and then ask yourself how you think the story of *Beowulf* fits into that framework.

Another major issue that confuses people when they read *Beowulf* is, "Is this a Christian poem or not?" That's actually a really interesting question, and one that you should keep in mind as you read. Remember the context in which the poem was written. The Saxons had taken over England, they were Christian now, and this is a story of something that happened several centuries before during the pre-Christian era. There are frequent references to Scripture, but only to the Old Testament, never to the New. Beowulf is clearly a noble hero, but not clearly a Christian. The poet is sympathetic with these people, but also doesn't paper over their flaws. At first glance you would think that Beowulf is cast as a Christ figure, but at the same time, there appears to be no ultimate hope in the poem. As you read, see if you can formulate an opinion of what the poet is doing with this.

There are a number of themes woven throughout this narrative that may need a word or two of explanation before you start reading so that you can better understand the poem. Keep these in mind as you make your way through.

In Anglo-Saxon society, the **Mead-Hall** was at the center of life. It was a huge feasting hall, and, as foreshadowed in the name, it was where mead was served (mead being a fermented honey drink). But it was more than just that. In the mead-hall, the warriors swore oaths of allegiance to their lord, and the lord gave treasure to his men. This giving of treasure was called ring-giving, and because of this, the king was called the **Ring-Giver.** His loyal warriors were called **Thanes.** When war broke out, as it frequently did, the bonds that held the men together were the oaths they had sworn in the mead-hall. They owed their lives and their allegiance to their ring-giver because of his generosity to them. This presents a really interesting concept of government, one that is very unfamiliar to us. For the Saxons, the king was the central giver and therefore the one to whom allegiance is owed. In our system, we give our money to the government because we owe them our allegiance. As you read, pay attention to this relationship, because it is foundational to the Saxon way of life, and therefore to the story of *Beowulf*.

Saxon life was tribal, and frequently there was trouble between the clans. Let's say two men from different tribes had a disagreement and one killed the other. The victim's clan would then come to retaliate, and because of the way the world always works, they would escalate the situation and kill (let's say) three of the opposing tribe as payment for their fallen friend. Then that tribe would feel deeply wronged, and would gear up and come to get some payback, and *they* would kill ten men as payment for the fallen three. You see the problem, I assume. These vicious cycles were called **Blood-Feuds**, and once a blood-feud had gotten under way there was virtually no way out of it aside from the two clans mutually exterminating each other. The blood-feuds were fueled by the Saxons' sense of allegiance to their comrades, as well as a system of morality in which **Vengeance** was seen as justice.

Sometimes, in the midst of a vicious blood-feud, there would be an attempt to pull out of it. A common method of trying to establish peace was by means of a **Peace-Weaver**. This was a woman from one tribe, who was given in marriage to someone from the opposing clan. The idea here was that the two clans would then be related, and would therefore call a halt to the killing. How often this was actually successful I have no idea, but the author of *Beowulf* is clearly very skeptical of the concept. Peace-weavers show up in a number of places in the poem, but always in a tragic role and without any hope that it's going to work out in the end.

When you consider the importance of the mead-hall, of loyalty, of avenging fallen comrades, it's unsurprising then to find out that **Kin-Killing** was seen as the ultimately grotesque crime. A man who killed a member of his own family had turned the universe upside down. He had killed one he should have died to avenge, he had become the enemy, and he had brought the blood-feud right into the mead-hall. The idea of the kin-killer is a major theme throughout this poem, and one to definitely pay attention to as you read. Try to figure out what the poet is saying when he brings this in.

One last note. The Saxon word for poet is **Scop**, pronounced "shope." We get our modern English word *shape* from this. A poet was a shaper, one who shapes with his words. A cool and somewhat profound link to this is that God is the ultimate Shaper, the one who shaped heaven and earth with His Word. For the Saxons, the role of poet was a very important one, because it mimicked God as Creator. Different cultures tend to relate to God in different ways and focus on different aspects of His character. The Saxons saw God fundamentally as Creator. He was the ultimate Scop. Because of this, they valued their own poets very highly, and saw them in the role of sub-creators.

First Fitt

Funeral of Shield

Hear the song of spear-Danes   from sunken years,
Kings had courage then,   the kings of all tribes,
We have heard their heroics,   we hold them in memory.
Shield Sheafson was one,   scourge of all tribes,
Took a maul to the mead-benches,   mangled his enemies.
He rose and in rising,   he wrecked all his foes.
A foundling at first,   he flourished in might,
A torrent of terror,   war tested his mettle.
So he bested and broached   the borders of nations;
10   The whale-road was wide   but his warriors still crossed it.
Gold came, and glory . . .   a good king that was!
So Shield had a son,   sent as a gift,
A cub for the courtyard,   a comfort from God
For the nation had known   long gnawing of troubles,
Great trials and tempests,   long times of deep suffering.
They were left leaderless   so the Lord of all Life,
The great glory-Ruler,   gave them a chieftain.
Shield's son he was,   and summoned for glory.
Beow was brilliant,   a banner of northernness,
20   The pride of great princes,   the pride of his family.
So warriors in warfare   must be wise in that way
As ring-givers rise   they reach their companions
So later in life they   won't be left on the field.

His thanes will stand thick with him,   there battle is joined.
Such generous gifts   are good for deep loyalty.
Shield was still strong   when summoned in time,
This Dane-king departed   to death—the Lord's keeping.
His thanes thanked his memory,   and thought a sea burial
Would keep the command   their king had passed on to them.
To the shore of the sea   they shouldered the burden,   30
Committing the king   who had covered his people.
Silent, sheathed in ice,   the ship rode the harbor,
The ring-prow was ready,   and rigged for the journey.
They laid out their lord,   beloved by all of them.
Amidships the mast,   they remembered and placed
Treasures and tackle   and trust most of all,
Battle gear, blades edged,   and bright gold and silver,
Prestige presided there,   piled honor on deck,
I never had known   a north ship so fitted—
The weight of that wealth,   and the warriors whose tribute,   40
Would sail with this ship   with it sent far away,
Their purpose presenting him   to the power of the flood.
They decked out his death,   and dealt with him bountifully,
No little gifts, no less   than left with him as a babe,
When set adrift on seas and waves,   a sent-out waif,
They left him lonely,   lost but for destiny.
They set high the standard,   a standard of gold
High toward heaven,   with hearts full of grief,

Here is a good synopsis of the Ring-giver / thane relationship

Notice what we are told about the burial of a king: Shield was piled up with treasure and pushed out to sea in his ship. He left this life the way he entered it, floating alone on a ship piled with treasure.

It's also important to notice that this story opens with the funeral of a king.

The ship they let slide   to sea it departed.
50 With minds full of mourning,   no man here can say,
No wise man, no warrior,   no wizened hall scop1
Can see or can say   who will salvage that treasure.

Second Fitt
Hrothgar rises, Grendel stirs

So Beow then built   some battle strong towers.
Admired and esteemed,   an able king for the Danes
Through a long life and rule   when left by his father
To his rule and reign   and his right to the throne.
Then his heir, the great Halfdane   held sway in his turn
As long as he lived,   their lord and their elder.
He was a father of four,   this fighter and chieftain.
60 One after another   they entered this world,
First Heorogar, then Hrothgar,   then Halga the good.
Then came a queen,   future queen for Onela,
A balm for the bed   of that battling Swede.
Then Hrothgar held firm,   held victory in battle,
Friends flocked to him,   foes fled,
And mighty grew his men,   a masterful army!
So a command came to him,   the king thought to build
A royal hall, rising in fame,   erected by guildsmen,
With gables and glory   and greatness forever,
70 A mead hall, a marvel,   for men to speak of forever.
There his throne would be,   and thriving with gifts,
He would give out those gifts,   all that God had bestowed—

Kingly gifts, but no common lands,   or cruel giving of souls.
This royal hall, as I have heard,   was a haven for craftsmen.
Through middle-earth, men were summoned,   making way to the building.
Soon it stood, magnificent,   and soon its glory rose.
Finally finished,   in full view it stood,
The hall of Heorot,   as he spoke the name,
The worthy king had willed it,   whose word was law.
So he kept his kingly word   and came with rings,   80
Treasures, and torques,   the tables were heaped,
The hall reared up high,   with horn-gabled corners,
Baiting the battle-flames,   that burning would come.
Hatred for Hrothgar   was held in abeyance
But a son-in-law soon   would bring samples of rage.
Now a demon demented,   in darkness a prowler,
Held a hard grudge   when he heard with great pain
The great and the good   with glory were feasting,
The scop sang their songs,   and the strings were well played,
The harp filled the hall,   a herald of joy.   90
So skilled in his singing,   he sang the creation,
The Almighty had ordered   the earth to be fashioned,
Shining, the single plain   surrounded with waters.
He summoned the splendor   of sun and of moon,
Lifting as lamps   their lights for earthwaru.[1]
He filled all the fields   with fruit for the tasting,
He gave us such greenery,   good leaves and branches,
And made man and beast   that all move in His quickening.

---

1   *Back-coinage from helwaru, meaning inhabitant of Hell.*

Note the use of "middle-earth," a common Saxon image which was picked up by Tolkien.

That's some ominous foreshadowing. They're only just building Heorot and we already are hearing how it's going to go down in the end.

Notice that the poet is singing about God as Creator. This was how the Saxons fundamentally related to God.

　　　　The place was full peaceful,　　and pleasant for men
100　Till finally a fiend,　　fresh out of Hell
　　　　Began to give grief　　with ghoulish, wild haunting.
　　　　This grim monster was Grendel,　　gifted with terror,
　　　　Haunting marches and moors,　　marauder of villages,
　　　　Malicious and miserable,　　in marshes he lived
　　　　For some time with the terrors,　　the type who were banished
　　　　By the Creator, as kinsmen　　of Cain, who had blood on his hands.
　　　　The Eternal Almighty　　had everlasting vengeance for Abel.
　　　　Cain had gotten no good　　from his grasping in envy
　　　　For the Lord of all life　　from the light drove the kin-slayer
110　And he went far from all friendship,　　into fens of dark exile.
　　　　He was the father of phantoms　　and far from the living,
　　　　Begetting ogres and elves　　and evil black ghouls,
　　　　Giants defying good Heaven　　again and again
　　　　Until the time came　　for the Titans' great judgment.

> *Grendel isn't just a horrible monster, he's a monster descended from the first kin-killer. We are supposed to see Grendel as the embodiment of kin-killing treachery. Notice that what upsets him is the joy and the fellowship in the mead-hall.*

Third Fitt
Grendel kills thirty, Heorot deserted

　　　　Quietly night came,　　and creeping, Grendel as well,
　　　　To spy out the safety　　of the soldiers' great mead-hall,
　　　　To see how they slept　　after savoring beer.
　　　　Great nobles were nodding　　and never disturbed,
　　　　Lost to sadness and sorrow,　　summoned in peace,
120　Dead in their dreams.　　The damned spirit came

suddenly,
Furious, fierce   and formidable in anger
Grim and greedy   he grasped thirty men
From their rest and he rushed   to the refuge of home,
Flushed in his fury,   inflamed in his hatred,
The bodies he butchered,   in bulk he took them.
The grim dawn's gloaming   light gave to disaster,
The depth of destruction   was done and forever.
Wails from warriors,   their weeping was heavy,
The morning for mourning,   their mighty chieftain,
So long their leader,   so lifted by grief.   *130*

That strong king suffered,   stricken with sorrow,
He thought of his thanes,   he thought on their loss,
Aghast at the ghoul's carnage,   grieving his men,
He looked on the loathsome tracks   left by the monster.
He was stunned, struck numb,   but severed from hope,
The very next night   their nemesis came back,
Striking again, slaughtering more,   savoring murder,
Malignant, malicious,   no remorse for his sinning.
So then the thanes shifted,   the thanes moved their bedding,
Seeking rest somewhere,   somewhere other than Heorot,   *140*
Sleeping in some of the   scattered outbuildings.

Who but the blind   would bed down in there?
Who could not conceive   that conqueror's deep hatred?
Whoever escaped   kept always away.
So Grendel in greed   held goodness at bay,

One against all,   that one against many,
Till greed toppled greatness.   The ghost hall, deserted,
Stood wasted twelve winters   of woes in their seasons.
The Shielding lord suffered,   his sorrows were deep,
150 In terrible torment,   his torment in grieving.
All tribes heard the telling,   and retold the lays,
Sad mournful music   of the murders of Grendel,
How Hrothgar was hated   and the hall was deserted.
The feuding ferocious,   the fighting was spiteful,
Nothing but war, nothing,   and nothing but battle.
No peace and no parley,   no peace-price accepted,
The Danes must all die,   he dealt nothing but anger.
No herald could hope   to hold an agreement,
Given as gift   by those gut-bloodied hands.
160 Instead the sick monster   would stealthily wait,

As darkened death-shadow,   a dim ambuscade,
Waiting for warriors,   a wicked hot malice,
On moors that were misty,   where men cannot know
How these whispering warlocks,   these wights from Hell glide.
So crimes he committed,   cruelties plentiful,
That fiend in his frenzy,   that fiend in his hatred.
He made Heorot his home,   haunting at midnight,
Ghostly and gliding   in the glittering hall,
But the thought of the throne   was a thought filled with horror,
170 He could not come near it,   because he was an outcast.
Heartbreaking hard times   were these held by the Shieldings,
Their princes, their planners,   their powerful

The Danes are called "Shieldings" not because they are so excited about their shields, but because they are descended from Shield.

counselors
Would come offer counsel   to their king in his grieving,
Plotting and planning   their path of resistance,
How best to give battle   with brave men and warriors.
Weary, they wavered at times   worshipping idols,
Summoning sacrifices,   saying old words aloud,
Praying the demon who damns   would deliver them.
Old customs were curious   but comfort was missing.
Their hope was in Hell,   and their heathenish ways,   *180*
In dire need and deep thoughts   they did not know God,
The Lord who loves justice,   the Lord judges our deeds.
The High King of Heaven,   the holiest one,
Was not known to them   though they needed his wisdom.
Cursed is the coldness   of comfort deceiving,
That thrusts a poor thane   in a thicket of fire,
Forfeiting help and forgiveness   forever.
But blessed is the man   who busy in prayer,
Can deal with the dying   and deliberately seek
The Father's great fellowship   and final protection.   *190*

Fourth Fitt
Hrothgar broods, Beowulf sails & meets Coast Guard

Now the action moves away from Denmark and over to Geatland and the court of Hygelac. See map on page 12.

In that troubled time   the trouble continued,
No stop to the sorrow   and steady affliction.
So soon Halfdane's son   had strife far too great.
Night terrors, night panics,   and never a respite
From the cruel spirit's spite   and sputtering envy.

But home in his haven,   Hygelac's thane,
A good man, a Geat,   had heard of Grendel's deep
  malice.
Strong-minded, the strongest   of all sons of men,
In his time, battle-tested,   he was tried and was ready.
200 High-hearted and huge,   he held out the order
To fit and to fashion   a famous wave-cutter,
To sail the swan-road   to serve the Dane king.

No sage tried dissuade   that savior from going,
Though dear and devoted,   they did not deny him.
They wrestled to reach,   they read all the omens.
That mighty man   had measured recruits,
The best from all battles,   the bravest of Geats,
Stalwart and strong,   the strength of their nation.
He tested and tried them   and told them his mission.
210 A captain courageous,   a clustered fifteen,
Skilled at the sea   toward the shore they went down.
The time quickly came,   the quest had begun,

The ship was soon set,   settled by cliffs.
Men soon gained the gangway,   their gear was then
  stacked;
The eddies edged the boat,   they entered with
  weapons,
All mounded amidships,   hard metal bejeweled.
They shoved off and sailed,   they sailed to their
  journey,
The sea willing and waiting,   the ship well-braced with
  timbers,
To open sea, across the salt water,   they accepted their
  task.

Hygelac is the most important character in Beowulf *to be historically identified in other sources (Gregory of Tours for one). Hygelac died in 516, which helps with identifying the time period for the story of Beowulf.*

The foam flocked her neck,   she flew like a bird   220
Till they came in good time,   at the second day out.
The curve of their cutting prow,   the carving of water,
Such that they saw land,   these seafarers sighted it,
Sunlit crags, silvery cliffs,   and shores with steep rocks.
Landfall at the headlands,   and a looming bright shore.
The deep sea was done,   that deed was behind them.
The voyage done, they vaulted the rail,   over the side,
And stood on the sand   and savored their landing.
They moored and made fast,   their mail flashed and clattered,
They thought to give thanks,   with thanksgiving to God   230
For a smooth and silent wave-road,   for a simple crossing.
A watchman waited,   a warrior of the Shieldings,
Whose duty was diligence.   Every day on the sea-cliffs.
He saw their gear glinting,   down the gangway they passed it.
His desire burned deep,   that devoted sentry,
Hrothgar's fine horseman   held his spear out,
Riding down at the ready,   they would reckon his challenge.
His manner was manly;   his message was formal.
"What has the wave-road brought us,   what warriors are you?
Your coats speak of combat,   your courage is open,   240
Glinting with gold,   must we guess at your purpose?
Your high ship is here   with your hull on our beach.
A sentry and sea-watch   stands silent for years,
Long have I held watch   as Hrothgar's eyes on the coast,

And never have known   such nobles to land here.
I guard against greed   with great armies behind them.
Never before, never so brazenly,   have boastful invaders
Carried shields to this coast   with questions unasked.
Have our kinsmen consented   to your coming this way?
250 And a mightier man,   massive and strong
I never have known.   He is no mere retainer,
Dressed in such dread   and deadly fell armor.

Your lineage, lord,   give me leave to request it,
Before leaving your boat   to begin your way inland,
I must know your mission,   your men and homeland,
You strangers and spies,   scouting out our own Denmark.
I ask then again,   this ocean brings aliens.
I seek what you say,   the sooner the better,
It is best to be brief   and before more time passes."

Fifth Fitt
Beowulf answers the Coast Guard

260 Their leader unlocked   the lid of his word-hoard,
And spoke words of silver,   summoning wisdom.
"We are Geats, of good will,   from a great, far-off nation,
Hearth-men with Hygelac,   that high-hearted chieftain.
My father was famous,   his fist was renowned,
Ecgtheow, eager for battle,   he entered true glory,
He went with his wisdom   after long winters extended.
All counselors, with their craft,   coveted his wisdom.

We still haven't learned our hero's name, but we do know what kind of character he is. The Saxons liked things to look like what they were. A mighty warrior should look like a mighty warrior and it should be obvious to everyone who sees him (the Coast Guard) that he is no ordinary man. Americans tend to like underdog stories. The kind where the wimpy kid in the back of the class turns out to be a ninja, or the kind where the funny little everyday hobbit becomes the unsuspecting hero. But this is not how the Saxons thought; for them, heroes needed to look like heroes. They weren't into surprise packages.

They knew him, and knowing,   they never forgot him.
Our hearts are not hardened,   we hold out good faith,
We come to your country,   your king, son of Halfdane,   270
Your shield and your shelter—   you should show us the way.
Our mission is not minor,   a message for your king,
That leader of leaders,   the light of the Danes.
No secrets, no spying,   we were summoned by trial.
Your terror, your trial,   that terrible night-bane,
Who ravages this realm,   who ruined your feasting,
Some sort of ghoul,   a seal on your grief,
With malice malignant   he murders your people,
In shame and in slaughter—   my service is offered,
To Hrothgar my heart,   my whole-hearted counsel.   280
A plan I propose,   with purposed deliverance.
Such counsel has come,   and keeping with prudence,
If Hrothgar will hear it,   he will heal from his sorrow.
If not he will never,   benighted and blind,
Get free of that fiend,   or follow deliverance.
That coldness and cruelty   will keep coming to haunt him
As the height of that hall   rises high up to taunt him."
Undaunted, decisive,   the deadly-eyed sentry,
Astride his great stallion   summoned an answer,
"With stout heart, and sense,   you can see right away   290
The difference, the distinction,   between doing and talking.
But I take your tale,   your troop is full loyal
To the shield of the Shieldings.   Let me show you the

way.
With your weapons of warfare,   you may walk here behind me.
My comrades commanded   to keep your ship safely,
Fresh tarred for the testing,   this trial, your mission.
They will hold it in honor,   unharmed from an enemy,
Until once again tested,   it tries the high seas
With curved prow courageous   to carry you homeward,
300 As heroes, high-hearted,   to the homes of your Geatland.
May your courage come with you,   and keep your lives safe,
The valiant, surviving,   and victory secure."
So they set off together,   and their ship rode the water,
Broad in the beam,   the best of their fleet,
Resting on ropes,   riding at anchor.
Boar-shapes in bronze   on their battle cheek guards,
Good were the goldsmiths   who gave them that fierceness.
Those warriors walked,   they went in formation,
Until coming closer   they caught sight of glory,
310 The high-timbered hall   that held their fell mission,
Both good and great,   the gilding was splendid.
Men knew what it meant,   and majesty lived there

The glint of gold roofing   gave out stabbing light.
Their guide, the sea-guard,   gave them instructions.
Dazzling but distant,   he directed them to it.
The shortest and straightest way,   simply to follow.
Then he wheeled and he went,   wished them Godspeed,

"May the great Father favor you   and find you in
   kindness,
Bestowing His blessings   and backing your exploits.
For myself I must go   and make my way back   *320*
To the coast where I can   keep my watch up for
   raiders."

Reading 2
Questions

Make sure you double-check your answers in the back of the book.

1. Look at the description of good old Shield Sheafson in lines 4-11. What sorts of things did he do? What kind of king did that make him? Be sure to take note of this as the poet is going to be doing something rather interesting with it later in the book. The phrase, "that was one good king" is going to be repeated later. Make sure you remember what it looked like the first time around.

2. "Ring-giving" is a major theme throughout *Beowulf*. Lines 21-25 describe the transaction that occurs between a ring-giver and his thanes (warriors). For a king, what is the purpose of treasure?

3. Think of the dragon's relationship to treasure in *The Hobbit*. What is the key difference between the way a dragon treats treasure and the way a good Saxon king treats treasure?

4. Hrothgar built an amazing mead-hall called Heorot. In lines 80-81, what goes on in the mead-hall?

5. After the description of the glory of Heorot, we get an ominous foreshadowing of the doom that eventually awaits the hall in lines 83-85. What is that eventual doom, and where will the problem come from?

6. What in particular upsets Grendel about the mead hall? (Lines 86-89)

7. When Grendel hears the song in the mead hall, what are they singing about? (Lines 91-98)

8. Who is Grendel's ancestor, and what was that person's crime? (Line 106) This is a very important feature of the poem and becomes a

prominent theme, so make sure you take note of it. Compare that person's crime to the cause of the eventual doom of Heorot. What is the similarity?

9. Can you think of any similarities between Grendel and Shield Sheafson?

10. The question of the role of Christianity in this poem is a very interesting one, and will unfold throughout the book. The poet is clearly Christian, but what do you make of the characters? What clues have we been given so far as to the state of things among the Shieldings? (Lines 91-98, 176-187)

11. We are introduced to our hero in line 194. So far he is nameless, but we know what kind of man he is. What does he look like? What does the Coast Guard think of him? (247-252)

12. Do you notice anything Tolkien is borrowing from Anglo-Saxon culture? Make a note of anything you see.

Sixth Fitt
Beowulf and Wulfgar

It was paved there, and perfect,   the path ran on straight.
The men in their mail,   marched glinting in sunlight,
Mail hand-linked, hardened,   high gloss in iron,
Which sang as they stepped,   straight to the hall,
All grim was their gear,   and good was their step.
They stacked all their shields,   these sea-weary warriors,
Holding that hardwood,   on the high wall they leaned.
The benches soon bore them,   their battle-dress clattered,
330   Their spears were soon stacked,   these seafarers' weapons,
Like a spinney of spears,   straight ash, true and gray,
With the troop no less true,   all tested in battle.
Then a proud noble probed   and put them a question.
He asked of their origins,   his opinion not hidden.
"Whence have you wandered   as warriors so fell
And brought all this battle-gear,   this bounty of might,
These shields, these spears,   these summons of death?
I am Hrothgar's herald   and his high-retainer,
And never have known   such nobility in wanderers.
340   Surely bravery or battle,   not banishment, brings you
To Heorot and Hrothgar,   to have such a presence."
Then man spoke to man,   as majesty would have it,

> *Here we finally get our hero's name.*

The great Geat leader   gave quick reply,
Hard in his helmet,   "We are Hygelac's men,
My name, bestowed at birth,   is Beowulf.
If that master of men,   most famed of kings,
High over all, Halfdane's son,   will hear me out,
I would be grateful to greet him   and give him my errand,
Make known my mission,   and make him aware."
Wulfgar then, prince of Wendels,   warrior renowned,   350
With wisdom well known   and a well-tempered spirit
Said, "I will serve as your herald   and seek out an answer
From our devoted Dane-king,   daring in battle,
That giver of gifts,   that great giver of rings.
I will question the king,   your quest announcing,
And bring back an answer   to beckon you to him,
The audience your entrance   has eagerly sought from him."
And the tall warrior, turning,   past the tables he walked
To where Hrothgar held court   at the head of the hall.
Gray-bearded, grizzled,   and grim in his majesty,   360
Solemn, surrounded by nobles,   he served face to face.
Wulfgar spoke to his sovereign,   he stood fast in the courtesies.
"These men are a marvel,   they made it from Geatland,
Sailing over seas   to speak with you now.
Battle-hardened, brave,   with Beowulf their leader,
Lord of the Shieldings, they seek   to speak with you now.
They want to have words,   they would have your ear.
My high lord Hrothgar,   you hold their request,
So do not deny them,   disappointment forestall.

370 These warriors are worthy,   their weapons are noble,
　　　Their bearing is brilliant,   their bravery outstanding.
　　　Mark their chosen chief   who chose such retainers."

Seventh Fitt
Hrothar & Beowulf meet, "Fate must go as it must"

　　　Hrothgar, Shield to the Shieldings   summoned reply:
　　　"Why, I knew this young noble,   and never forgot that boy.
　　　His father, justly famous,   was fated as Ecgtheow.
　　　Hrethel the Geat gave him   the gift of his daughter,
　　　Such that their son   is here seeking out friendship.
　　　It is time to determine   the tests of old loyalties.
　　　Some men, merchants it was,   made their way to the Geats once,
380 To carry gifts for the giving,   graven presents and thanks.
　　　They were sent back with stories.   The strength of thirty
　　　They said was stored   in the strength of his hand.
　　　Now holy God in His goodness   has guided him here,
　　　In His manifest mercy,   in His manifold kindness,
　　　To desperate Danes   to defend us from Grendel.
　　　Send him in, send him in,   summon him quickly,
　　　I will truly offer him treasures   for his tested courage.
　　　I hope in his heroism,   I will hand him great bounty.
　　　Go now and get him   and gather him quickly.
390 Bring him. Our barons   will boast to have met him.
　　　Greet them warmly and worthily,   tell them welcome to Denmark."
　　　Wulfgar went to the door   and welcomed them

Beowulf's reputation preceeds him.

heartily.
"My lord, the leader of Danes,   your lineage knows
And says that your surety   is strength in your battles.
He salutes your seafaring   and summons your courage.
Come in, come in,   and come in your armor,
Wearing helms to see Hrothgar,   and Heorot bids welcome.
Your spears must be stacked,   your shields must remain
Until kingly counsel   has concluded this matter."
That hero, high-minded,   held silent and rose,   400
With him thanes powerful, potent,   and part of them stayed
To watch the weapons   as their warrior chief directed.
Their prince led; they proceeded   and passed through the door
Into Heorot's haven   with a brave-helmeted leader.
He strode forward and stood   to speak with the king.
Then brave Beowulf spoke,   bold in his armor,
Chested in chain-mail   the chosen smith had woven—
"Hail to Hrothgar!   May good health not leave you.
I am from Hygelac's hall,   a strong help in his battles.
Many and mighty were youthful deeds   offered my   410
  master in days past.
Then news of Grendel to Geatland came,   grim were the tidings.
Sailors told stories   of your suffering people,
How this great and good hall   lies ghostly and empty
To your warriors once evening comes,   once the sun has set
And the light lowers its way   below the lip of the world.
All our elders advised me,   our wise men gave counsel,

Saying I should sail,   cross the sea to your service,
Offer help to you, Hrothgar,   give help to the Danes.
They never had known   a naked strength greater,
420 Had seen me bloodied by blows,   but battling through it.
I beat down and bound   some beasts, five in number,
I took out a troll-nest,   I tackled sea monsters
On the water and waves,   drove warriors from Geatland
Who honestly asked for it.   I was eager to do it.
Undaunted I drove them,   devastating them quickly.
And so against Grendel   I give out my challenge,
To settle that score   in single combat.
So Shield of the Shieldings,   grant this single favor—
Having come this far, do not refuse.   My ferocity simmers,
430 Bold king of the Bright-Danes,   their bravest defender.
Grant me this gift,   ring-giver and king,
That I have the pleasure to purify this,   the palace called Heorot
With my men, masterful all,   I mention no others.
I have heard this hard monster   uses no help from weapons,
Reckless, scorns to submit   to the swordplay we use.
To heighten Hygelac's glory,   that his heart may be gladdened,
I renounce sword and shield   and will serve you bare-handed.
I will waive this thick war board   and will wage hand to hand
My fight with that fiend   and will finish his story.

Beowulf tells Hrothgar of some of the monsters he has killed in the past. We know that Beowulf is good in battle, but in this poem he is primarily known as a monster-killer.

Notice what Beowulf promises here: to fight Grendel bare-handed. He also tells us why he's going to do this.

Foe against foe,   I will fight for us all.   440
Death comes, one will die,   he will deem it God's justice,
Who settles and summons   His servants inscrutably.
If this ghoul Grendel wins,   he will gruesomely devour
The Geats in that grim hall,   and will gobble them down
As he done, as he has devoured,   those dead in your war-hall.
My face won't be favored   with a final death covering,
He will carry me cold,   no comfort will greet me,
As he, gorged and gloating,   will run to ground to devour me.
My body all bloodied   will be battered and torn,
Will be food for that fiend   as in a frenzy he eats me,   450
Fouling his fetid nest   as my final chapter.
No laments, no long mourning,   no lays to be sung,
No funeral is fitting,   no final rites or observances.
But if battle bests me,   Hrethel's brilliant war shirt
Should be reverently returned   from this retainer to Hygelac—

Wyrd is the Saxon word for fate, and of course Weland is the name of a Norse god.

Weland wove it.   Wyrd must go as it must.

Eighth Fitt
Hrothgar's speech and welcome

Hrothgar, helm of the Shieldings,   held forth as he spoke,
"Beowulf, brave friend,   bringing the best of help,
Out of kindness you came,   with the comfort of strength.
Your father once fought,   and a great feud erupted   460

When he killed and conquered   that capable Heatholaf,
A warrior among Wulfings,   with his own hand.
The wantonness of war   was wending its way,
And fearing, his folk shunned him,   and forced him to leave.
Undaunted, he came to the Danes,   and dwelt here with us,
He wrestled rolling waves to come,   he witnessed our kindness
And the South-Danes served him   as true sons of honor.
Unused to rule, I was a young king then,   yearning to grow,
Establishing sway over strongholds,   and settling the wealth.
470 Heorogar, son of Halfdane,   did not hold to life.
Elder brother and better man,   in battle he went down.
I sent wergild to the Wulfings,   over the water I sent it,
And Ecgtheow acknowledged me   and accepted strong oaths.
It burdens my breast   to believe that I must
Reveal the wreckage that   rivalry with Grendel has wrought,
What havoc, what humiliation,   what hell he has brought us.
My ranks have been ravaged,   my realm has been weakened,
Fate has not favored us,   fighting is futile,
Swept by a strength   that is stronger than all of us.
480 But God can take Grendel,   and use a good man to do it.

Hrothgar tells Beowulf of his relationship with Beowulf's father.

Wergild means "man-payment": money paid to the relatives of a killed person to prevent a blood-feud.

Time after time   when the toping was strong,
Strong thanes thought to meet him   and thickened in courage
Said they would slay him   and summoned their ale-strength
To be heroes in Heorot,   to be hailed in the mead-hall.
They sharpened their swords   and silently waited.
But daybreak and dawn showed   their dark blood on the floor,
Slick and sickening,   blood spattered on benches,
My following faltered   and feasting diminished.
Tested and tried   we were all taught to fear.
Now sit to your supper   and seek to untie your thoughts,   490
Great warrior, give to us,   gifts as you desire."
Then a bench was brought,   a bench was cleared
For the Geats to gather,   together to sit down.
In courage they came   quite proud in their bearing.
A servant was summoned   and served out the mead-ale,
The gold pitcher was good,   the good ale was brighter.
The scop would sing,   his song filled the hall,
A herald of hope,   and Heorot was glad.
The gathered men were glad,   both Geat and Dane.

Ninth Fitt
Unferth and Beowulf clash

Not everyone is happy Beowulf is here.

Crouching by the king's stool   was a crafty man,   500
Unferth, son of Ecglaf,   undone by envy,
Carping, he spoke contrary   to the coming of Beowulf—

Sea-bravery, strength in battle,   sickened that man,
Who, vicious and vexed,   had his vitals eaten by envy.
He would not grant greatness   to other good men,
Under heaven he held   that all honor was his.
"Beowulf? who challenged Breca   in boats on the open sea?
That rowing test was risky,   your rivalry great.
In pride you proceeded,   you proved you were boastful,
510 Risking the deep, no restraint,   if reckoned in pride.
Foe or friend,   no facts could dissuade you,
Both of you boasting,   your boats in the water,
Stroking, boats swimming,   you slid from the bay,
Embracing water, eager,   you entered the trial,
Manic and mulish,   you measured the sea-roads,
Riding swells of the sea,   which swayed like your pride.
The winter waves rose,   and wild was the rowing.
You toiled in the tempest,   you took seven nights,
Driven by desperate waves,   the deep almost took you,
520 In that contest he conquered,   came to shore victorious,
Washed to shore by the sea,   safe near the Heathoreams.
He belonged to the Brondings,   and back he returned,
To the place he preferred,   becoming prince to his people.
So Breca, son of Beanstan,   has bested you fully,
Fulfilling his future,   your fears have been realized.
No matter your mettle   has been measured in battle,
Your battles and bouts,   your belligerence tested,
If you dare to defy him,   this demon of Heorot,
You'll die to greet Grendel,   this ghoul in the hall."
530 Ecgtheow's son answered,   the utterance of Beowulf,

Unferth is clearly threatened by Beowulf's presence, and for good reason. Unferth is one of Hrothgar's thanes, and it's humiliating to have an outsider come to solve their monster problem. The obvious question is, why are Unferth and Grendel both still alive? One of them should be dead if Unferth had been doing his job. Unferth is trying to discredit Beowulf by telling this story of how he was defeated by his friend in a rowing competition. If he can't even beat Breca, how can he expect to conquer Grendel?

Now Beowulf gives his version of the story.

"Unferth, you utter just words,   Unferth my friend,
Your beer talks of Breca,   it's beer wisdom I hear.
The truth is more telling,   I can tell that adventure.
I had more strength for the stroke,   though the seas were hard.
I held up under hardship,   in high waves and water.
As boys like to boast—   as boys we grew up—
We decided to do it,   and we did as we said.
The ocean was open,   open, inviting,
We dared to defy it,   however daunting it was.
With swords to serve us,   we shoved off from the beach.   540
The sea roiled, we rowed,   with real steel to protect us
From whale beasts in winter,   from watery monsters.
Breca couldn't break from me,   his back bent to the rowing,
Nor could I pull away past him,   though powerfully stroking.
Shoulder to shoulder   we struggled five nights
Until the deep drove us,   divided us finally.
The wintery waves,   the wicked cold drove us apart,
The perishing north wind, pointed,   pounded us fiercely,

Again we see Beowulf fighting monsters.

Dark night, deep waters,   stirred the deep creatures,
Agitated and angered them,   all of them wild.   550
My chain mail, chosen well,   was choice for that battle,
Hand-forged, hard-linked,   it held up against them.
A woven war-shirt,   worked with gold,
Covered my courage,   encasing my heart.
A sea-dragon dragged me   down to the deep bottom,

Pinned and pinioned,   my point finally reached him,
My sharp sword drove in,   I stabbed as I could.
That battle blow reached him,   that sea beast was slain,
A hungry, huge monster   my hand finally conquered.

Reading 3
Questions

Make sure you double-check your answers in the back of the book.

1. In lines 322—331, what do you notice about the poet's description? Which of our senses is he appealing to?

2. It's not until line 343 that we learn this hero's name. His name is a kenning: *Beo* means "bee" and *Wulf* means "wolf." When you hear the kenning "Bee-Wolf" what would you guess the meaning is?

3. What sort of battles has Beowulf already had? (Lines 421-422)

4. How does he intend to fight Grendel, and why? (Lines 434-438)

5. Who will decide the outcome of the battle according to Beowulf? Compare line 442 to line 456. Do you see any conflict? What do you make of that?

6. In lines 459-473, we find out that there is another motivation for Beowulf to come to Hrothgar's aid besides his desire for glory. What is it?

7. At the feast in the mead-hall, what motivates Unferth to speak?

8. Do you notice anything Tolkien is borrowing from Anglo-Saxon culture? Make a note of anything you see.

Tenth Fitt
Sea creatures, Unferth silenced,
vow to Wealhtheow

560 Again and again   angry creatures rose up,
Lurking and lunging.   I lashed with my sword,
My battle blade served me,   I bested them all.
My sword-feast, their sorrow,   they suffered my blows,
Dark things from the deep   who would devour me happily
On the sunken sea bed,   savaging my bones.
In the morning these monsters,   mangled and pierced,
Asleep from my sword,   were softened and rotting
Like so much dead debris,   destined for nothing.
I brought safety for sailors,   with those sea monsters dead.
570 Light lifted the east,   light covered the land,
The bright beacon of God,   a balm for the seas.
Then I saw sea-cliffs,   the shore of the headlands,
Those windswept walls.   Wyrd often delivers
The doughty and daring   if dauntless he stands.
And so I now summon you   to seek out such a tale,
When nine sea-beasts were nailed   in fierce night battle,
Killed by my craft,   killed dead with my sword.
Near death, desolate,   on the deep I floated,
How I came unharmed   from that hostile brood,
580 How I lived to see light   the Lord only knows.
Though spent with the struggle,   the sea brought me,

Beowulf washes up on Finland. This means he was on the Baltic Sea side of Geatland.

On the flood with the flotsam,   to Finland's coast.
Now I don't hear such deeds   being dealt out to
  Unferth,
Your boasts—and Breca's—   have such battle not seen.
Your swords were not celebrated,   not seen in such
  straits,
Or for facing such fights   on the field of battle.
Not to boast of my battles,   I bested my enemies.

Here we find out something very important about Unferth—he is a kin-killer. Beowulf also wonders aloud why, if Unferth is so awesome, is Grendel still alive?

But your kith and kin   were killed by your hand,
Your closest kinsmen,   the curse of Hell waits,
Corrupted by cruelty,   however clever you are.   590
I tell you the truth,   you true son of Ecglaf,
The grim deeds of Grendel   would not have gotten this
  far,
That malicious monster,   your master distressing,
Wrecking havoc in Heorot,   if your heart for battle
Were as bold as your boasts,   that beast would be dead.
But he finds no feud from you,   no fierce rush of
  swords,
No dread of the Danes,   no death from your weapons.
He vaunts over Victor-Shieldings,   his vicious glee
Takes his tribute,   he tastes his spoils
In the land of lost Danes,   in his lust for the kill,   600
He kills, he consumes;   no counterattacks
From stalwart Spear-Danes,   no strength in response.
But I will soon show him   what strength is made for,
The pride and power of Geats   will prove the point to
  him.
After battle, brave to mead,   the best may go,
When the sun rises soon   on the sons of men,
And the light lifts his face   to lighten our way."
The treasure-giver took hope,   he tasted it now,

White-bearded, war-brave,   he had waited long.
610 That Bright-Danes' best prince   from Beowulf heard
The first hope, firm hope,   and with fisted resolve.
Then loud laughter came   from liegemen rejoicing
With words that were winsome.   Then Wealhtheow entered,
Hrothgar's high queen,   heeding all courtesies,
Greeting these guests,   gold-arrayed and lovely,
That high-hearted lady   handed the first cup
To the conquering Dane-king,   the cup filled to the rim.
She bade him the best;   the beer was golden.
He was lauded and loved   in the lives of his people,
620 So gladly she gave it,   he gladly received it.
The Helmings' high queen   in the hall walked regally,
Carrying the cup,   that queen was their servant,
Offering up mead   to all elders and youths,
Til that royal-ringed woman,   rich beyond measure,
Came to brave Beowulf   with the beer in her hand
And greeted the Geat lord   and gave thanks to God,
Speaking wise words.   Her wish was fulfilled
Through a hero to hope in,   through a hero in truth
Who came bringing comfort.   The cup he received,
630 That warrior was welcomed   by Wealhtheow's hand.
He spoke serenely,   though seeking out combat.
Then Beowulf spoke brave words,   the best son of Ecgtheow,
"My thanes and I thought on   the thickness of battle
When we entered the ship   and embarked to the ocean.
To fight to the final,   or fail in the attempt,
Was the work we wanted,   and the will of your nation.

The queen's role in the mead-hall is to serve the mead to the warriors.

So I am firm for this fight   and the fiend's grip will take me,
Or I will take him and test him,   or my tale ends here."
That woman was well-pleased   having witnessed his valor,
This battle-heart of Beowulf,   this boast of a good man.   640
Bright in gold, beautiful,   emboldened she sat
By Hrothgar her husband,   in the hall both presiding.
As before, brave words spoken   with bustle and chatter,
Warriors' great words   wafted upwards like smoke,
A confident company   until it came time for bed.
Hrothgar, son of Halfdane,   was heedful of rest,
For he knew that the night   would bring nothing but battle,
A fight with a fiend   in the festival hall,
When the great shining sun   was seen no longer,
And the darkness, deep darkness,   brought the demon to haunt them,   650
And shadowy shapes   came slinking around.
The warriors, all weary,   rose well-ready for bed,
Both leaders took leave,   good luck for the moment,
Hrothgar held out his hand,   and hailed the young warrior,
Gave him the hall,   the wine-hall to guard it.
"Since shouldering my shield,   since sheltering my people,
Never before   have I bound the hall over
To the hand and the heart   of another high warrior,
Except now to such   a great servant as you.
Recall and remember   resplendent glory,   660
So watch for that wicked one,   no wish will fail you

If you conquer and kill him,   if you come through alive."

Eleventh Fitt
Asleep in Heorot, Beowulf trusts God

Hrothgar, hero-king,   and his house-guard departed.
Shielding king, shelter of the people,   sought his rest
With his best bed-comfort,   his bride queen Wealhtheow.
The conflict was coming   but the King-of-Glory
Had set a guard against Grendel,   that grim marauder,
So men heard of the heroics   of the hall-defender,
Who guarded the great king,   with good intent.
670   In truth he trusted   the tested strength of his arm
And in the goodness and greatness   of God over all.
He took off his tunic,   his trusted iron corselet,
His head unhelmeted,   he handed his sword
To his selected steward—   that sword was the finest—
Told him to guard the gear,   the gear from his battles.
Then Beowulf, before that man   bedded down
Gave out a great boast,   good although proud,
"In a fight I hold fast,   no feebler I am,
Than Grendel the grim   would grant for himself.
680   And so with the sword   I do not seek to fight
But his life I will lift from him,   that lies in my power.
He knows nothing of war-craft,   no knowledge of the arts,
No shield work or sword play,   though his strength is great.
We both are bold,   so in battle tonight

This is a noticeable moment. Hrothgar leaves and goes to bed with his queen, leaving his hall to be defended by a foreigner.

Beowulf lays aside his weapons. Grendel doesn't fight with a sword, so neither will he.

We shall spurn sword work,   if he seeks me here,
With no weapons for this warfare.   Let only wise God,
Our living Lord,   lift His countenance on one
And decree the doom of it   as He deems right."
The chief reclined and rested,   his right cheek on the
  pillow.
His noble head nodded,   night came.   *690*
His sea-roving sailors   sank to rest on their beds.
None thought that survival—   the night thickened with
  danger,
From hall-floor to home,   thoughts hurrying on
To the land they loved—   would lead them back!
Full well they knew warriors   were wasted by Grendel,
Death seized many Danes   in the dreaded hall,
But conquest and comfort   were coming to them—
God's war-loom was weaving   to Weders this victory.
He gave greatness to one,   a grip of deliverance,
A single man's strength   to save all the people.   *700*
The truth can be told now,   this tale of deliverance.
The Most High, His majesty   weaves marvels for men.
He always rules over men   in Almighty wisdom.
Then down through the darkness   the demon
  approached,
The shadow-stalker came,   stealthy and vile.
The guards were slack, sleeping,   silent, unconscious.
All but one, Beowulf,   that brave deliverer, who knew
Into darkness the demon   could not drag any man
Apart from the providence   of the perfect God.
One man was masterful,   a mind filled with battle.   *710*

Twelfth Fitt
Grendel is disturbed and advances

Out of the marsh, by misty crags,   the marauder crept.
Grendel, under God's wrath,   came greedy for blood.
The bane of brave warriors,   emboldened and turning
Toward the high hall,   hungry for flesh.
Under mist, in the murk,   till the mead-hall he spied,
He came in his cruelty—   the hall crafted in gold,
Weary yet wonderful,   a witness to joy.
This, Hrothgar's home,   a haven for nobles,
He had battered before,   but his bane waited now.
720   The hall held great heroes   and hard luck for Grendel.
Lost and alone,   that lost soul kept coming.
He crept as he came,   and crushed the great doorway,
With fisted, great fury,   and fire in his stomach,
Boiling in blood-lust,   he burst out in anger.
Door hinges were hanging,   he hastily entered.
The bright patterned pavers   he polluted by walking,
He stood, then he strode,   anger streamed from his eyes,
Flamed, then flashed,   like fire it was.
In the hall heroes slept,   he hungered to see them,
730   Kinsmen and clansmen   all clustered and sleeping,
Lieutenants and liegemen.   He laughed in his malice,
For the monster had mind,   before morning could come,
To savage each soul,   to sink his teeth into them,
Greedy and gluttonous,   Grendel was ravenous,
And wanted his way,   but wyrd put a stop to it.
Never after that night   would he knead a man's bones.

Watching and waiting,   the warrior from Hygelac
Watched the cursed killer,   and counted the seconds.
How the monster would move,   making his play—
Not that the were-shape would   wait very long!   740
Straightway he seized   a slumbering warrior,
His first prey, and fiercely   he fisted the carcass,
Bit him down to the bone,   his blood he drank greedily,
He grabbed him in gobs,   and gobbled him down.
In one moment the monster   had mashed and devoured him,
Both feet and both hands,   and blood on the floor.
He walked toward our warrior,   to welcome the second,
Extending his talon   to take up another,
But Beowulf, boldly,   bested his reach,
Propped up and powerful,   prompt in response.   750
Then that sin-shepherd   soon saw far more trouble
Than he ever encountered   in all middle-earth,
In marshes, on moors,   the might of such strength,
Such a heavy, hard hand-grip,   his heart started quailing,
Perturbed and then panicked,   powerless to run!
He recoiled, retreating,   he wanted to run to
His devil den.   This dealing was new,
He never had known   such knocks in the old days.
Then brave Beowulf,   his boast fresh remembered,
Surged in his strength   and strained all he had,   760
He grasped his foe firmly,   whose fingers were cracking,
The giant got off,   the great man soon followed him.
With eagerness eating him,   the monster intended
To flee, to get free,   and to fly far away,
To take flight to his fens,   his fingers were slipping

In the grip of that grim one.   No good was this trip
To the great hall of Heorot,   no happiness here.
Timbers rocked and the racket   revealed the great tumult,
The Danes heard the din,   and the daring could listen
770 To the ultimate beer brawl,   that battle careened
From wall to wall,   the wonder was the hall stood.
The fighters were furious   and fought all in,
The timbers shook, but stood,   the struggle continued,
The strain of that struggle,   sustained, taut,
Threatened the thick beams   but throughout it stood,
Held within and without   by wide iron bands,
Cunningly crafted,   but they continued crashing
Through many mead-benches—   men still talk of it—
Glistering with gold,   for all the grim foes cared.
780 The way they wracked it,   the wisest Shieldings never thought
That any man, or ogre strong,   or eager warrior
Could hurt or harm   that horn-tipped hall—
Only torching fire could touch it,   only terror hot
With scorching smoke,   could soon bring it down.
A roar redoubled,   and redoubtable Danes
With fear were filled,   with frenzied panic,
Standing guard at the garrison,   hearing Grendel's howl.
That hellish howl   was heard by everyone,
The cry of that captive,   his clamor and pain
790 Was heard down in Hell.   Beowulf held him,
Stalwart, stubborn,   the strongest of men,
Who ever earned honor   under the sun.

Reading 4
Questions

Make sure you double-check your answers in the back of the book.

1. Beowulf says in line 582 that after his epic rowing contest with Breca he washed up on the shore of Finland. Look at your map on page 12 and locate roughly where that adventure occurred.

2. As Beowulf finishes answering Unferth, he adds a personal detail which gives us a clue as to the kind of guy Unferth is. What do we find out about him? (Line 587) How does that tie in with the theme of the poem?

3. Beowulf also makes sure to point out that Unferth and Grendel are both still alive. What does this imply about Unferth?

4. In lines 663-665, we see Hrothgar leaving the hall for the night. What do you think of the king leaving and going back to his bed? What does this tell us about Hrothgar?

5. Do you notice anything Tolkien is borrowing from Anglo-Saxon culture? Make a note of anything you see.

Thirteenth Fitt
Fight with Grendel

That earl-warrior was eager   to see emptiness take him,
To catch this night caller—   this killer must die,
His life was no loss,   his liberty shaken
By a mighty man.   Now many Geats
Flailed in fury   with their finest swords,
Protecting their prince,   their power tremendous,
But all of their blows   bounced off his hide.
800 They had not known,   nearing their enemy,
These hardy friends, heroes,   these high-hearted warriors,
Swinging their swords   from several sides,
That the keenest blade could   not kill the creature.
The best blade on earth   would bounce off harmlessly,
Not hurting or harming   that hideous beast.
Safe under spells,   from swords and from weapons,
From edged wrath and iron.   Yet his end was upon him,
His life was soon leaving,   his lights were flickering,
His passing was painful,   his passion was agony,
810 His descent to the devil   was discovered as loathsome.
He who had harried men   and hated their joys,
Hostile to holiness,   his heart feuding with God,
He had murdered many   and men greatly feared him,
But his frame failed him,   this fiend lost his grip.
Hygelac's hero,   that high-hearted warrior,
Held death in his hand grip,   his hold was tremendous.

We find out here that swords can't harm Grendel. So even though Beowulf renounced weapons purely for the glory of killing him bare-handed, it turns out that it was the only way he could kill him.

Each one of them hated   that the other one lived.
That creature then cracked,   his cruelty rewarded,
His broad shoulder burst,   and bloody sinews popped,
Those bones were broken.   To Beowulf belonged   820
The glory that was given,   and Grendel was driven
To his den, to his death,   in the dark marshes waiting,
In the fens' filthiness   he was fleeing in sorrow
To the end of his ugliness,   to the end of his life.
The desire of the Danes,   their dearest wishes,
Were fulfilled in fierce battle   by the finest of warriors.
Their rescue from ravages   was wrested in freedom
For Hrothgar's hall.   The heroic and wise warrior
Had purged its pollutions.   He was pleased by his
    work,
His devotion and deed.   To the Danes of the east   830
His boast was believed,   his bravery delivered
Them from sadness and sorrows,   their sickness in envy,
The bane of this battle   they had borne for too long,
The pain and pollution,   the passions of hatred.
The proof of proud victory,   presented in gladness,
When the hard warrior's hand   held the grim trophy,
The talon he tore off,   with the torn arm and shoulder,
And Grendel's long grip   to the gable was nailed.

Grendel's arm was hung from the ceiling.

Fourteenth Fitt
Giddy retainers, story of Heremod

Many came in the morning,   this marvel to see,
Gathering at the gift-hall   to gawk at the trophy,   840
Clan chiefs coming,   compassing great distances,
Along wide, wandering roads,   in their wonder
    discussing

> The monster's fell footprints.   His fatal departure
> Did not give them grief,   that grim flight recorded
> By the trail of tracks,   and the tale it told.
> Despairing, the demon   had disappeared,
> Wracked and ruined,   to the wretched monster lake,
> Doomed and despairing,   he dragged bloody footprints.
> The blood boiled in the water,   bucking and seething,
850 Swirls of hot wound-slurry,[1]   surging in turmoil,
> Oozing out envy   and utter disaster.
> Facing his death-fate,   his fen then received him,
> Lurking, and luckless,   from life he relinquished
> His hard-hearted soul.   Hell came then and took him.
> Spirits high, singing,   old soldiers and young ones,
> Rode home on horseback,   hailing the hero.
> Beowulf's brave deed   was blessed and applauded
> By well-mounted men,   by men beyond joyful.
> They praised and praised more,   they persisted in saying
860 That far north or near south,   between nether seas,
> In the whole world,   no warrior was better,
> Under heaven's high sky,   no heroic shield-bearer,
> Would ever win more   and be more worthy of rule.
> But they laid no blame on their lord,   they left him alone,
> Hrothgar was held blameless.   What a good king that was!
> At times the good men galloped   their gray horses racing,
> Released and running   when the road was straight,
> And the path and the place   were perfectly well-known.

Grendel's bloody footprints lead back to Monster Lake.

This is a very interesting comment from the poet. He goes out of his way to tell us that no one blamed Hrothgar. We also once again hear the phrase, "What a good king that was."

[1] This magnificent kenning is Seamus Heaney's.

The scop is singing of this great feat, and he tells stories of other famous monster-killers as well. Sigemund killed a whole clan of giants and then eventually a dragon, bringing great treasure to his people. Sigemund was a figure in Norse mythology and his story is told in much more detail in the Völsung *Saga. It's a pretty wretched story, full of incest and general bad deeds.*

And song after song   the scop would recount
From his storehouse of stories,   singing with wisdom,   870
Glorying in good words,   the great, ancient tales,
One after another   he eagerly sang them,
Weaving in wisdom   old words with new ones,
Praising Beowulf's power,   and proving his talent
With a lay and well-fashioned lines   that lifted up fame.
Braiding his best words   with the best deeds of men.
He sang of the strength   of Sigemund's arm,
His fame and his feats,   and fearsome marvels,
The wandering of Waels' son,   the wide roads he traveled,
The foul deeds and feuds   and fighting unknown,   880
Except to Fitela, his friend,   who would never forsake him.
When he desired to discuss   these deeds with somebody,
They were nephew and near-uncle,   they both knew the stories,
As battle-friends, brave together,   they brought enemies down.
Conquering they killed   a whole clan of giants,
Seeking with swords   to signal their glory.
After the day he died,   undimmed was his glory,
Because Sigemund had slaughtered   the serpent, that dragon,
That taker of treasure,   that taster of gold.
That great prince under graystone   gave the dragon the point,   890
Daring and dauntless,   and doing it alone,
He saw the grim serpent,   and his sword went home

Through the shining scales   of the serpent and dragon,
Who was pierced with the point   and pinned to the wall.
That dragon died.   The daring of his slayer
Meant he had mounds   of magnificent treasure.
The son of Waels wasted no time,   weighed down his boat,
All the hold could hold,   and it held a great deal.
He carried dazzling treasures down,   before the dragon then melted.

900 He was famed as a fighter,   his ferocity unmatched,
A baron of battle,   the best in the business.
His great and good deeds,   all gained by his courage.
King Heremod faltered in health,   his campaigning slowed,
His valor was vanquished,   victory lost to the giants.
Betrayed by black moods,   backed into a corner,
He met death, deserted,   deserving no better.
His sickness and sorrow   had sunk his people,
With despair, disappointment,   and death for his nobles.
Experienced men damned that expedition   in those earlier times,

910 Who knew that nobility   should not bring affliction
From haughtiness, hubris,   and hollow arrogance.
They proposed that a prince   should protect the people,
Prosper the people and nation,   and preserve them from danger,
Taking title and treasure,   but not to torment them,
That homeland of heroes,   the home of the Shieldings.
Beowulf was better,   and believed to be better,

Sigemund is praised, but then the scop moves straight into telling us about Heremod. Sigemund killed a clan of giants; Heremod was defeated by giants. Sigemund killed a dragon; Heremod was a dragon. As we find out later, he hoarded his wealth and would not give treasure to his men—just like a dragon.

Here Beowulf is contrasted with Heremod, as he will be again later.

> *Hrothgar arrives on the scene, with a bunch of women. The poet obviously wants us to notice this—but remember that he told us that no one blamed Hrothgar. "What a good king that was."*

Heremod was harried,   hollowed out by sin.
Still racing, rejoicing,   the retainers paced their horses,
On the sandy and single road   that sent them all homeward.
Well after daybreak, delighted,   doughty warriors   920
Gathered to the gift-hall   to see the great marvel.
The king himself came,   from the queen's quarters,
Regal and royal,   the ring-treasure guardian,
Well-known and noble,   knights and earls with him,
A column of comfort,   the queen right beside him,
And beautiful, bountiful,   a bevy of women.

Fifteenth Fitt
Hrothgar views arm, Beowulf wishes he had corpse

Hrothgar held forth,   on the hall's steps he stood,
Under steep eaves, standing,   sure-footed, regal,
With the roof garnished in gold,   and Grendel's great claw.
"For this fine sight—finally!—   I cannot fail to thank   930
Sovereign God with submissive thanks.   Our sorrows were plenty,
Both raids and wrath,   and ruin from Grendel, but
God gives wonder after wonder,   the wise herder of glory.
Not long ago I had lost   any lively hope,
Weighted with woes   and wasted in grief.
I thought as long as I lived   I would be lost in this misery,
With blood staining the stones   of this stately great house.

Wise men withered in counsel, the woe had no relief,
We had no hope of hindering this hellish marauder—
940 Infernal foes and fiends found their way nightly,
Harrowing our hall. Through this hero now,
By the wisdom and work of God, this wonder is done,
Which all of our wisdom would not work for us.
For Beowulf's bravery, blessed among women
Is she who bore this bairn, who brought us our freedom.
To the sons of men I say, if she still lives,
That the God of all goodness was great through her.
Now, Beowulf, best of men, in battle triumphant,
As a son I laud and love you, lift your name high,
950 Keep this new kinship, carry it with you,
Acknowledge and nurture it, know that it's yours.
All worldly wealth here I would gladly give to you.
For lesser victories, lesser men, largess has been given,
From my hoard in this hall to honor lesser achievements,
By men less stout and steadfast. You surpass them,
Fulfilling your fame in all future ages,
Your name will be known and nobility remembered,
If the God of goodness gives recognition to you."
So Beowulf, son of Ecgtheow, spoke in response,
960 "This was a willing war, a work that I sought out.
I have fought the good fight, and faced down this devil.
But I wished for a greater win, with Grendel, whipped and dead,
Lying defeated and dead, devastated on this floor.
My strategy had been to seize, and in my strength to pin him down,

To grapple that grim demon,   and with my grip to kill him.
I planned to pin him down,   hold him powerless,
Until that brute should breathe his last—   but he broke free.
I could not keep him—   the Creator did not will it—
His panicked hatred I could not hinder,   and he hid deep in the night,
My lock on his life slipped,   but he left a token behind!   970
He ran and in running   vain rescue he sought.
He left his curdled cruelty,   his claw and shouldered arm,
Left behind, bleeding;   my boast is nailed there.
That wicked wretch   ran wailing off
And won't live long,   that loathsome criminal,
Sunken in sin,   with sorrow astride him.
Death's grip has grasped him,   he has been grabbed by anguish.
Though sadly my grip slipped,   I say Death's will not,
Guilt dripping, blood drying,   his doom approaching,
Whatever Majestic wisdom means,   whatever the   980
Maker doles out."
The son of Ecglaf was silent then,   his speech was stopped,
All his boastful words of bravery,   his battle-prowess talk,
Since the nobles all had noted   not one of them was greater
Than that hideous hand   on the high eaves nailed,
Gigantic fingers grim,   those gray-clawed spikes,
Like burnished steel, bent spikes,   short spears for infighting,

Savage, wicked sharp,   and seething with rage
Though dead, deadly,   though done with fighting,
That uncanny claw terrified.   It was clear to all of them
990 That no man's blade or bravery   could battle through that hide,
However sharp, no sword   could sever that thing,
That bloody battle-claw   from that beast full of hatred.

Sixteenth Fitt
Heorot refurbished

The command soon came   to reconstruct the hall,
And all hands were assembled,   and all pitched in with a will.
Wise men and women   the wine-hall restored.
The tales found in tapestries   were told from the walls
With golden good woven in,   and the guest-rooms refurbished,
The splendor was shining again,   the scene magnificent.
Though braced with bands of iron,   though bolstered with metalwork,
1000 The building was broken,   battered and ruined,
Hinges were hanging loose;   the hall roof alone
Was sound and safe,   unscathed by that monster's flight,
When bloody and beaten,   he fell back in his panic,
Despairing and dying,   his destiny pursuing him.
No man runs from that ruin;   we should realize that now.
Each soul, all souls,   every one of us with breath
Must make our way   to the maw of death,

All men, sons of middle-earth,   must make our solemn way.
Our bodies on the bed of death,   after the banqueting of life,
To that destiny come in death,   which deals the final round.   *1010*
The hour came for Halfdane's son,   and the hall received him,
For the king came in   and called them all to feast.
I have never heard such a host   in happier noise,
No group more graciously gathered   around a giver of rings.
The benches were bowed   under the battle-warriors' weight,
Round after round   of the royal mead passed.
The mead-cups were many,   and mighty men drank them.
Hrothgar and Hrothulf   were in high spirits,
Powerful kinsmen came together,   close in friendship.
Heorot was full of friends,   at least for present.   *1020*
Betrayal and treachery   had not yet been tried.
Then Halfdane's stalwart son   gave a standard to Beowulf,
A gift fashioned from gold,   a guidon of victory,
An embroidered battle pennant,   a breastplate, a helmet,
And a splendid sword   which many saw presented.
It was borne to Beowulf,   and best honored that triumph.
He gracefully received the gifts,   and good they were,
And Beowulf drank deeply there,   no dishonor was present.

More ominous foreshadowing about the eventual doom of Heorot.

I have not heard   of any heroes so honored,
1030 With fantastic gifts, cunningly fashioned,   and four of them,
A silvered mead-bench ceremony,   solemn and glad.
On the raised ridge of the helmet,   the ridge was prominent,
Wound tight with wires,   and was warden and sentry,
Lest an assault from a sword   should strike the wearer
And it go sharp in the strife   when with shield he went forth
To fight with his foes   and find them in battle.
Then the king commanded   that a cluster of horses be brought,
Eight of them in all,   embroidered with gold on their bridles,
Their handlers brought them into the hall—   one horse was decked out
1040 With a saddle set with jewels,   studded, resplendent;
It had been Hrothgar's   when high-hearted to battle
He used to go to adventure   when eager swords clashed.
His courage in combat   never cowered or quailed;
He was daring and doughty   when dead bodies fell.
The honorable Ingwine king   gave authority to Beowulf
Over these weapons and war-horses,   and wished him wise in the use of them,
Bidding him to steward his bravery,   the best way in fighting.
So the Danes' leader and lord   led them in gratitude,
Dispensed from his hoard to the hero,   and

Here we learn that Hrothgar had been a mighty warrior once, and he's exemplifying the ideal king here as he shows himself to be a very generous ring-giver.

handsomely paid him
With horses, high treasure   and humble acknowledgement   *1050*
As those who love this tale will tell—   the truth is obvious.

Reading 5
Questions

Make sure you double-check your answers in the back of the book.

1. Why were Beowulf's men useless in the fight with Grendel?

2. Lines 864-865 contain an interesting commentary on Hrothgar. What do you make of them? What do you think the poet is saying? We get the line again, "What a good king that was." Where have we heard that before, and what's different about it here?

3. Lines 1019-1021 continue an ominous theme that the poet has mentioned before. What are we to expect sometime in the future, and how is that a part of the theme of the poem?

4. Do you notice anything Tolkien is borrowing from Anglo-Saxon culture? Make a note of anything you see.

Seventeenth Fitt
Beowulf rewarded, "Lay of Finn" begins

The king then came,   as custom decreed,
And gave the companions who crossed   the cresting seas with Beowulf
Great heirlooms and honors—   gifts to the ale-bench with him,
Precious and priceless gifts;   and paid the penalty, the wergild,
In gold for the one Grendel ate,   that grim repast,
A foul murder; many more   would have met death
Had not the wisdom of the wise God   deflected their wyrd,
Through that brave man's mettle.   The Maker and Creator
1060 Rules mankind by measure,   and means it for good.
Therefore, think ahead always,   thoughtful preparation is best,
Forethought and foresight   forestall worry of mind.
Since woe and weal fill up   this world of troubles,
Through the length of life's battles,   which linger long enough.
Then melodic music   mingled in the rafters,
When for Halfdane's heir   the harpist played,
Stroking the strings   and singing a lay.
The bard woke battle-joy   in the best men on the mead benches
When he began the stirring song   of the sudden raid

Remember that wergild is a ransom payment to fend off vengeance. Hrothgar had paid the wergild for Beowulf's father earlier, and he is paying it again now—assuming that since Grendel, their monster, had killed one of the Geats, the Geats might have sought vengeance against the Danes.

The scop begins another song, this one a story about Finn. This part of the Beowulf poem is known as the Finnsburg Episode.

> And assault on the settlements   of the sons of Finn.   *1070*
> Halfdane's great hero,   Hnaef the Shielding,
> Was to fall stricken, fated,   in that Frisian combat.
> High-hearted Hildeburh   did not hold in honor
> The Jutes and their jealousy.   Judge her innocent—
> She lost loved ones,   and lost on both sides,
> Her grown boy and brother,   they both suffered death,
> Struck by spears—   her sorrow was deep.
> Keening, not without cause,   she kept up her lament.
> None doubted Hoc's daughter   could see the dawn's
>   bloody greeting,
> When under the unforgiving sky   she understood   *1080*
>   death,
> Murder claimed her kinsmen,   and kept her in sorrow,
> All her peace and pleasant things   passed from the
>   world.
> Just a few followers   with Finn were left,
> And he could not conquer   or quell Hengest's men,
> Those warriors with weapons,   so more war was
>   fruitless—
> His remnant unrescued   by his right arm.
> A pact of peace he offered,   parleyed to terms—
> The Danes could dwell there,   done with fighting,
> Sharing high-seat and hall   and half authority,
> Joined with the Jutes,   and justice agreed upon,   *1090*
> Shared giving of goods   and gladness together.
> Folcwada's son saluted   and summoned great gifts,
> Favored Hengest's folk   with fabulous rings,
> True treasure given,   and torques bejeweled,
> And splendid gold, and silver,   stores of wealth.
> To spur the fighting fealty   of Frisians was first in his
>   mind,

Hildeburh is a peace-weaver, but the blood-feud between the two clans appears to have continued anyway. She loses her loved ones on both sides.

Hildeburh is a Dane and is married to Finn, a Frisian.

Pay attention to Hengest. You'll see him again later in the year. Keep an eye on his behavior in this episode.

They try to make peace after the fighting, and Hengest (a Dane) is given many gifts.

His own tribe, as tales say, as told in the alehouse.
So the pact of peace produced the strongest bonds,
Firmly held a final peace. Finn to Hengest,
1100 With oath upon oath and honor committed,
So the wretched remnant would reckon it wise
To be nobly ruled, no hatreds, so none of these men
By word waken trouble or work evil resentments,
Or in malice of mind mention their grief
In forgetting the feud that felled their chieftain,
Lost, rudderless, leaderless, that lot was their fate.
But if some foe of a Frisian fought with taunting words
To call back the cruelty, then come what may,
A sword must settle the doom summoned to come.
1110 Oaths were enacted and ancient treasures
Were brought from burial places and bound the vows.
The great Shielding, good warrior, was given to the pyre.
The pyre was placed well, and plain to see,
With gilded boar, battle helmet, and bloody mail shirt,
And hard warriors, high-hearted all, all held by death,
Slain in the slaughter, with the sword cut down.
Hildeburh wailed for Hnaef, and her son as well,
Bidding his body be brought alongside,
That his bones might burn, and his body ascend,
1120 Alongside his uncle, to the unfeeling sky.
Her grief song was great, grim wailing ascended,
With the smoke of the slain and death songs mingling.
The fire was fierce, the fallen consumed,
Brains boiling over, blood gushing from wounds,
The bodies bursting, the burning fire greedily ate

They try swearing oaths of friendship.

The Danish prince, Hildeburh's brother, was killed during the conflict. Hengest has now taken over his command. Hildeburh is mourning her brother and her son who are being burned together.

And gone were their great ones,   their glory vanished.

Eighteenth Fitt
Hengest plots revenge, Wealhtheow plans

Throughout the winter, Hengest and crew are the guests of Finn. You can imagine this being a fairly tense situation. Remember that Hildeburh has already lost her brother and son in the fight.

Those heroes were homesick,   and hungered for Friesland,
Their friends were fallen   and families far away,
Their homes and hearths   were havens long missing.
Hengest held on   through the hard and long winter,   1130
Keeping a prisoners' pact,   and powerless to sail
And point his curved prow   to the pleasures of home,
Over wintery waves.   Those waters were rough,
Either lashed by long storms   or locked up in ice.
He sojourned there, simmering,   waiting springtime's arrival,
Bringing welcoming warmth   to the waiting of men,
With the sun in the sky,   the long season over.
The fields were fair,   full was the spring;
The guest of Finn gathered   that good was the time
To sail, but silent in thought,   he sought out vengeance,   1140
Which his passion preferred   to plowing the seas;
Wanting his hatred to hasten   the heat of vengeance,

Hengest snaps, and rather than returning home, decides to violate all his oaths of peace and friendship. He murders his host Finn.

Wheeling his wrath   on the unwitting hapless Jutes.
And so the time for treachery   tempted him by rising
When the high sword Hunlafing   was held in his right hand,
The brightest of blades   was brought to his lap.
Feared by the Frisians,   its finest edge was known.
He struck Finn, slaughtered him,   stabbing him through

	Under his own roof, an ugly death by sword took him.	*So now Hildeburh has lost her husband as well as her brother and son. Hengest loots the place, and takes the treasure and Hildeburh back home, but for her this was a despairing homecoming. She lost everyone she loved on both sides.*
1150	For Guthlaf and great Oslaf the grim attack had told	
	In sorrow and sadness after their sea voyage,	
	Lamenting their losses and losing their joy.	
	The wretched hall floor reddened and reeked with blood.	
	Finn was killed, cut down, his companions slaughtered,	
	Clansmen and king together; his queen was seized.	
	She was borne to their ship, the Shieldings took her off	
	With the chieftain's chattel, they chose their plunder.	
	They found and fingered all of Finn's treasures,	
	Whether gems or jewels or just the gold.	
1160	With the fabled fair queen a fair breeze took them	
	Over the deep to Daneland, her despair going with them.	
	The lay and lament finished, the loud feasting resumed.	*The poet immediately turns and brings Wealhtheow into the story. She walks over to an uncle and nephew. (We just heard about an uncle and nephew being burned on the same pyre because of a blood-feud.) In the middle of the uncle-nephew group is Unferth, noted for kin-killing.*
	Bright clamor commenced, and cupbearers hustled,	
	With wine in white flagons. Wealhtheow then rose	
	To go in her golden crown where two good men were sitting,	
	An uncle and unfailing nephew, each one true to the other,	
	Persistent in peace. Pale Unferth was spokesman,	
	Sitting at the Shielding's feet, his spirit was known,	
	His courage unquestioned, though his kinsmen had felt	
1170	The force of his ferocity when fighting broke out.	

Wealhtheow speaks optimistically about how kind the family will be to each other after Hrothgar dies. Given the context, the poet clearly wants us to hear the ominous music in the background. We were just told the tragic tale of a peace-weaver, and then we are shown a peace-weaver, hoping everything will turn out all right.

The queen said to the king,   "This cup is yours,
Great-souled giver of rings,   and good in your kindness,
Giver of gold to men;   to the Geats now speak
Such kind words of comfort   that kings should use.
Be generous to the Geats,   bestow gifts that are worthy,
Recall what came to you,   when kind gifts came your way.
I have heard it said in the hall   that you hold this warrior
In esteem as an heir.   This eager one purged Heorot,
Bright bejeweled ring-hall,   the best of halls,
So consider while you can   how to come with great gifts   *1180*
To please your people   before passing on
To greet your great judge.   For gracious I consider
My Hrothulf, high-hearted,   ready to hold rule
Now over young noblemen,   if that long night you enter
Before him, high prince of Shieldings,   haling farewell to us.
I consider him kind   and I call him to mind;
To patiently repay   these parents and their sons
For their honor and help   that they held out for him,
Their gracious gifts   and their giving of honor!"
She then came to the seat   where her sons were seated,   *1190*
Hrethric and Hrothmund   with high honor seated,
With good and great noblemen,   the Geat was there too,
Brave Beowulf   between the two brothers.

Nineteenth Fitt
Gifts bestowed on Beowulf

She carried a cup to him,   with kindness greeted him,
With gold-wire winding   and words that were winsome.
She offered two-intertwined bands,   torques for his arms,
A mail shirt, magnificent rings,   an immense collar of gold,
Larger than any left in these days,   no man alive has seen greater.
Such treasures were taken up   and talked about ever since—

1200   I have never heard of such a hoard   since Hama carried off
To his shining city   that solid Brosing necklace,
Encrusted with custom jewels—   now encrusted with hate,
Earning from Eormenric   only enmity and spite—
But worth it in worldly terms.   The Weder Hygelac,
Son of Swerting's son,   had that shining necklace with him,
Under his banner, in battle,   his booty defending.
But fickle is war, and wasteful,   and so wyrd overwhelmed him,
That time when he taunted   the terrors of war
To fight with the Frisians.   Fair ornaments and jewels

1210   He carried, costly gems,   over the curling waves,
Tempting fate, testing wyrd,   he tried death in his armor.
That king fell to the Franks,   fatal the battle,

Wealhtheow gives Beowulf an enormous collar of gold, which reminds the poet of the collar of gold that Hygelac (Beowulf's king) was wearing when he died in battle later.

They took that torque,   his trappings and chain mail,
The weaker warriors   the warfare carried,
From the blast of battle,   that bane of Hygelac,
And held the fatal field.   The festivities resumed.
Wealhtheow said to the warriors,   "Wear this well—
This treasured torque,   please take it with our gratitude,
And this breast plate, Beowulf,   well-beloved friend.
May you prosper in privilege,   and profit in life!   *1220*
May your strength be savored,   but to these striplings here,
Kind counsel that carries them.   I am concerned to repay you.
You have done such deeds   that in days and years to come
Your fame will flourish,   forever your honor will stand,
As far as the circling seas,   and the surge against the cliffs
And the headlands holding them.   May you hold your honor well,
O prince, may you prosper   with this pile of treasure
Live blessed and beloved.   To these bairns of mine
Show compassion, kindness,   and concern for their gladness.
Here everyone to all the others   is only and forever true,   *1230*
Mild in manner,   to their master they are loyal.
The thanes are all thoughtful,   the throng is compliant,
Beer-flushed and brave,   their boast is obedience."
Then she went to her seat.   The splendor of that feast was great;
The warriors had much wine.   Wyrd was not yet

Wealhtheow again is hopeful about how well they all get along. She wants Beowulf to remember her sons in kindness.

upon them,
Although many of those men   would their mortality own
After nightfall, never waking,   and never seeing the sun again.
Hrothgar stood high,   and home to bed he went,
Countless men, careful to guard,   were quiet and vigilant
1240 In the royal hall, their resting place,   they rolled their bedding
Between the benches,   set bolsters and pillows.
One beer-man in the banquet hall,   no less brave than the others,
Under his doom and his danger   went to death in that sleeping.
They were buttressed by bucklers   by their beds, at the head,
And their bright body armor;   on each bench there was set
In plain sight, polished,   their proud battle-helmets,
Their spears, their shining mail,   their swords at the ready.
Ready for combat, as custom decreed,   they came to their rest,
Ready for battle, ready for war,   not relinquishing care,
1250 Whether home by the hearth,   or harrying the foe
As wandering warriors,   as wyrd would have it.
They stood to serve their king—they were solid men.

Ominous. It seems that every happy moment in this poem ends on a sour note.

Remember that because of Grendel, the Shieldings have had to abandon the mead-hall at night. Tonight the warriors are staying, for the first time in years, but Beowulf is sleeping elsewhere.

Twentieth Fitt
Grendel's Mother kills in Heorot

They all sank into sleep.　But sorrow was stalking
The sleep of one soldier—　as so often happened
When Grendel guarded　that gold hall at night,
An evil ogre,　until his doom fell on him,
His payback and penalty.　It was plain at dawn
That a surviving avenger　killed the vicious ghoul,
And the word was worthy　and wise the report.
Grendel's mother, grim beast,　a ghastly dame,　　　*1260*
A mother and monster,　mourned her loss.
In the dread water, wet doom,　she dwelt for centuries,
In the cold depths of cruelty,　since Cain's time,
When he slew with a sword　his sole brother,
Surviving his father's other son:　spurned he fled,
A marked man　with murder on his hands,
He wasted in the wilderness.　There went out from
　him
Such ghouls and grim beasts　as Grendel, who preyed
On human flesh and human souls,　and at Heorot
　found
A waiting warrior　watching for a fight,　　　*1270*
The monster sought to maul,　with his mighty strength
　he seized,
But that man remembered　his might and his grip,
The great gift　that God had given him.
He trusted in the true God,　and took the mercies of
　God
As comfort and courage,　and conquered his foe.
That fiend then failed,　and fled the fall maimed,
Wretched, he ran　to the realms of death,

That enemy of men.   But his mother now,
Hungry and grim,   would go on a rampage
1280 Of grief and grim hate,   eager to avenge her son.
Up to the hall of Heorot   where high-hearted Danes
Were sleeping, secure,   and soon she burst in,
Turning the tables,   a terror in the night,
That monster's mother.   A measure less, though,
Was her terror told   as in the tale of battle women,
Amazons, women in mail,   than of men in arms,
When, hilt in hand,   the hammer-edge swords
Cut through the crests   of curious boar helms,
Blades wet with blood,   and battle-tested.
1290 Hard blades in the hall   in every hand were gripped,
Swords and spears at the ready,   shields lifted,
Tight and tough they stood,   no time for helmets
Or woven chain warrior shirts   when they woke to that
  assault.
When that demonic dam   was discovered she fled
To save her sorry life   when seen by the thanes.
She caught up a companion,   in cruelty and malice,
And fled toward her fen,   firmly clutching her victim.
For high-hearted Hrothgar   he was held as the dearest,
The finest of fighters,   with fame across seas,
1300 Whom she slew as he slept,   a slumbering hero.
Brave Beowulf was absent,   his bedding and housing
Were held in a house   with highest of honors,
After the gold was gifted   to the Geat for his prowess.
Heorot was in high uproar;   the hand-claw she
  recognized,
Blood-covered, bone out,   and she bore it off.
Grief in the hall was great   and no good was that
  transfer

Grendel's mother is the blood-avenger and comes as the embodiment of Vengeance.

Gendel's mother leaves with Grendel's arm and one of the men.

Where the good king and the Geat   had to give up
  bitterly
The lives of dear loved ones.   The lord of the Danes,
The great, gray hero,   with gravid soul
Saw his soldier gone,   slaughtered in malice,   *1310*
Departed and dead,   and a desolate king behind.
Beowulf was brought,   beckoned in haste,
His deeds not yet done.   As daylight spread,
He came with companions,   a company of earls,
To where the wise king waited,   worrying of fortune,
Wanting the World-ruler   to wield a better turn,
To take this miserable tale   and turn it to good.
He strode over stone pavers,   to the sovereign Beowulf
  came,
With his hearty and hale companions—   the hall's
  floors echoed—
Coming to greet the gracious king   with goodly words,   *1320*
Asking the dear lord of Danes   if the dark has passed
  well,
If slumber was sweet   and a salve to his mind.

Reading 6
Questions

Make sure you double-check your answers in the back of the book.

1. The poet's story in this section is known as the Finnsburg Episode or the Lay of Finn. Who is the center of this story? What are we, the readers, meant to focus on?

2. The portion of the poem immediately following the Finnsburg Episode is quite striking. What is the poet doing? How is he doing it?

3. With the entrance of Grendel's mother, the poet is doing some more interesting things with the theme of kin-killing and revenge. What are some of the ways these themes are showing up?

4. Do you notice anything Tolkien is borrowing from Anglo-Saxon culture? Make a note of anything you see.

Twenty-first Fitt
Hrothgar despairs and talks

1323 High-hearted Hrothgar spoke,   helmet of the Shielding,
"Don't ask of delight,   our doom has returned,
The dread of the Danes,   and death to Aeschere,
Whose younger brother was Yrmenlaf...   yesterday.
My rune reader,   my reliable adviser and sage,
A shield at my shoulder   in the slashing of battle,
When warriors fought   and we warded off blows,
1330 Our boar-crests bashed others,   and battle was hot.
I wish all my earls   were as Aeschere was.
But in Heorot an evil hand   hated and murdered him,
A ghastly and ghoulish monster   grabbed and took him off,
She pounced, proud,   and pursued her escape,
Full of her feud-lust,   filled up with vengeance
For the death that you dealt   and did it in strength,
When in your grasp, Grendel   gave up on life.
You knew the night terrors,   you knew how my thanes
Had been ravaged and wrecked.   But ruined and conquered,
1340 He fell before you.   Now fatal cruelty comes,
With fury and ferocity   the feud to continue,
Seeking revenge, seething,   settled on blood.
These thanes will think   in deep thickness of grief
Their ring-giver is gone,   a good man is dead.

The victim of Grendel's mother was Hrothgar's friend and advisor.

This is hard on our hearts.   A hand lies in death
That once won these men   with willing gifts.
Land-holders and lieutenants   who live in these parts,
Say they have seen   several of these things,
A pair that imperils   any poor souls out on the moor,
Border-stalkers, black strength,   and born for haunting, *1350*
Wandering wights,   wailing ghouls,
And from the tales told   one taller, one less,
One wraith a woman,   the other wicked, accursed,
In man-shape, a monster,   across marshes and meres
He slipped quietly, silent,   skulking through bogs,
Larger in life than men,   through long ages this
    Grendel,
Rural folk named and feared him,   his father
    unknown.
His line was woven in wickedness,   among wolves and
    ghosts
And demons and devils,   desolate was their home.
They wandered cruel crags   and cliffs at the headlands, *1360*
Fetid fens,   and foul the streams
Which cold from the cliffs   came down through the
    rocks,
Choosing underground chambers.   The choice is
    plain—
Not many miles from here   the mere spreads out,
And the edge of the frost-bound forest   fans out over
    black water,
The roots are rugged,   and wrestle the shore.
On clear nights uncanny sights   go cold to the bone,
The water burns and blazes,   that bog smokes.
Our people have not plumbed   the perils of that deep.
Desperate, chased by dogs,   a deer will stop short, *1370*

Rather than run on,   he reels and turns,
Surrenders his soul   stopping to die,
He gasps and gives up,   rather than go in that lake.
That gulf is no good—   Godforsaken.
When the wind works up,   the waves arc and toss,
The clouds stream and scud   when storms brew,
And that filth sags and surges   and soon enough,
The holy heavens cry.   Our help is now
Again with your good arm.   Will you go
1380 Unperturbed to that unknown place,   that place of fear,
To that sin-drenched silence.   Seek her out if you dare—
A warrior's reward   is warranted by battle,
And treasure, twined gold,   torques with jewels,
Your wisdom rewarded   if you win your way back."

Twenty-Second Fitt
Pursuit of Grendel's Mother

Bold Beowulf replied,   that brave son of Ecgtheow,
"Sovereign king, do not sorrow—   it seems better to me
To finish the feud   as friends wrecking vengeance
Than sorrow in silence.   We simply decide
To abide and endure   and exert valor always,
1390 To find dignity in death.   When his days are all done,
The worthiest warrior   is well-remembered.
Arise, royal king,   let us realize glory,
And tail the tracks   of this terrible mother.
I give my good word,   she will not get away,
Not in the high hills,   or hidden in forests,

Or on the floor of the flood,   her flight is all vanity.
But aged king, endure!   Await this great outcome,
With patience, empowered,   to push through these troubles."
That good and gray king   thanked God for His help,
Help merciful and mighty,   through that man's great promise.   *1400*
So Hrothgar's great horse   was handled and saddled,
A courser with curled mane.   The king rode ahead,
Resplendent and royal,   his regulars came after,
Shields on their shoulders.   She left clear footprints,
Wide and deep through the woods,   with signs easy to track,
A path clear and plain,   where she pressed and went through
The marshes and moors,   Murder under her arm,
She bore the best thane,   the brave Aeschere,
He who with Hrothgar   the homeland had ruled.
Then the proud prince   passed by the crags,   *1410*
Down steep defiles,   and deep under cliffs,
Narrow, unknown,   the noble king led them,
Past crags with caves,   crags with trolls.
At the front he fared,   a few men with him,
Searching for signs,   seeking the trail,
When he saw suddenly   on the slope above,
The tendrils of trees   tangled on the cliff face,
And a wood filled with woe.   The water below
Was bloody and black.   The brave Danish cohort,
Faithful friends,   and fearless Shieldings all,   *1420*
Bore bitter heartbreak,   the brunt of it there,
For Aeschere's honored head   was abandoned there,
Was found on the fell,   that fatal place.

That lake surf was surging,   the Shieldings saw it,
Heavy with hot blood.   A horn, lonely, sounded
A brave battle-cry.   That band paused . . .
They watched the water;   they saw worms and serpents,
Sea-monsters strange   that sounded the depths,
And cold and cruel kraken   on the crags basking.
1430   Morning light moved them,   the monsters departed,
Went on watery roads,   wandering off,
Whether distant or deep,   their dangerous way.
Hearing the horn,   those hateful beasts dove.
The great prince of the Geats   grasped his bow,
And shot with sure aim,   the shaft flying true,
Its mark a great monster,   striking its middle,
The sharp battle bolt   bloodied the water,
As the serpent swam slowly,   singled out by death.
The barbed boar-spears   with blows repeated
1440   Hooked and held him.   Hard death seized him,
Diving down,   still dragged to the shore,
A wondrous wave-wanderer.   The warriors gazed
At the beast before them.   Beowulf prepared
His war gear and weapons,   withstanding temptation,
Lest he fear to lose   his life to that creature.
His wide mail shirt, woven,   in the waters protecting,
Could best guard his body,   his bones safeguarding,
Lest the clutch of that cruel one   should crack him open,
And have his heart,   held with talons.
1450   The helmet for his head   was high protection,
And was soon to sink   to that swamp bottom,
Entwined with ten jewels,   as in times long past,
A smith had slaved on it,   and served it up glorious,
A wondrous work   by a weapon master.

> *This is strange. Unferth offers Beowulf his sword Hrunting to take down into the Lake of Monsters with him. He appears to be sorry now for his rash speech when he first met Beowulf. Even weirder though, Beowulf accepts, and they trade swords. We're told it's a good sword. But the only thing we know for certain about Unferth is that he is a kin-killer, and he presumably did it with this sword.*

It was bold in its boar forms,   so that no battle frenzy,
Could bite that bright helm,   believe it or not.
Unferth was another   who offered him help,
Hrothgar's servant and spokesman   a sword offered up,
A hilted sword Hrunting,   the heft was glorious,   1460
Of ancient heirlooms,   easily the best.
Iron at the edge,   with eager, deadly patterns,
Blood from battle tempered it,   brave for a fight.
No hero who held it   ever had to retreat,
When attacking, advancing,   invading the homeland
To face the foes   and fight fierce warriors.
Don't think this daring task   was destined as its first.
Unferth, son of Ecglaf,   was not eager to fight,
Though stout and strong,   and that speech he had uttered,
When doused in drink,   had departed from him,
That single swordsman,   less strong than the other.   1470
Under the watery waves   he would not bet his life
As a loyal lieutenant,   so he lost his fame and glory,
A boast not lost by Beowulf,   the bravest of men,
Who gathered his gear   for the grave encounter.

Twenty-Third Fitt
Beowulf Fights Grendel's Mother

Brave Beowulf spoke,   battle-son of Ecgtheow,
"High heir of Halfdane,   hold this in memory,
Great gold-giver,   now that I go down to fight,
What was said is settled,   sovereign and king—
If killed in this cause,   if that comes to pass,
If I lose my life,   be loyal still!   1480

> Do not fail as a father, be a father to me.
> Guard these good men, this gathering of thanes,
> These battle-brave men, if this beast should take me.
> And the gifts you gave me . . . give them a safe return,
> May Hrothgar give to Hygelac that handsome treasure.
> The Geat king will gather by the gold without measure,
> The son of Hrethel will stare and see those riches,
> And gather a good ring-giver gave famous treasures,
> And I rejoiced in the jewels and the gems while I could.
1490
> Let Unferth enjoy the iron edge I leave to him,
> Wave-edged, woven by smithies, woven while molten—
> With Hrunting I hunt, in hellish descent
> To a deserving destiny, or death will get me."

With these words the Weather-Geat prince,
Impatient with peace, plunged boldly in the mere.
The waiting water enclosed him, welcoming his dive.
It took most of the morning before making the bottom,
Before he felt the floor of that lake.
Soon he sought out that savage mother,
1500 And she sensed right away some man was raiding her lair,
She who had for one hundred winters held this domain,
Sensed the assault, and sought to grasp him.
So she clutched and clawed, when close he approached,
Seized the strong warrior to strike him with talons,
But his mail-shirt held his heart secure,

Beowulf asks Hrothgar to take care of his men if he's killed. He also asks that his treasure be sent back to Hygelac, and he specifies that Unferth can keep his sword.

As the she-devil strained   to slaughter-pierce,
The links in leather,   with loathsome claw.
Then this watery wolf,   when she touched bottom,
Dragged to her den   this doughty lord of those rings,
While he sought and strove   his sword to draw,   *1510*
To wield that weapon   against weird sea creatures
That beset him savagely—   sea-beasts assailed him,
With sharp tusks they tried   to test his mail,
They swarmed him, swimming.   Then he saw
He was in some hellish hall,   holding off the water.
He was where water couldn't reach,   no waves could drown him,
A vaulted roof reached up,   restraining the flood,
That furious froth.   Firelight guttered,
A flickering flame,   a faint but clear blaze.
Then he saw that she-devil,   that savage wolf-in-the-water,   *1520*
That monstrous mere-hag.   With a main stroke
He spun his strong blade,   and struck her foul head.
The blade sang as he swung,   a savage war-song.
But the battle-torch would not bite,   the brave warrior found
The sword failed to strike through,   the stroke failed to pierce
Or harm that black heart;   the hard blade failed
This man in much need,   yet marvels had wrought
In war hand-to-hand,   helmets cleaving,
Delivering death   to doomed men.
This was the first failure   befalling that glory-blade.   *1530*
But brave Beowulf stood,   not buckling in fear,
That high-hearted one,   Hygelac's kinsman,

Hrunting was undefeated—until now. Swords don't appear to work on Grendel's mother any more than they worked on Grendel. Beowulf has to discard it.

Rejected that wretched sword,   though richly embellished—
That thane threw it down,   thought to leave it there,
Though strong, made of steel.   His own strength he trusted,
His hand-grip of hard might.   So high-hearted men should do
When they want to win   the warfare brought to them,
Not tangled by troubles,   or tension or fears.
He grabbed the great shoulder   of Grendel's foul mother,

1540

The great Geat war-lord   grasped combat fully.
Filled with great fury,   he flung down that monster,
And that deadly demon   was brought down to the ground.
She twisted and turned   and took him down too,
With her ghastly grasping,   she grappled with Beowulf.
Spent with the struggle,   he staggered and fell,
Though fierce among fighters,   he fell nonetheless.
She chose his great chest   as a death chair; she sat,
Drew her great dagger,   and down it plunged,
To avenge his last victory,   the victim, her son.

1550

The braids linked on his breast   bested death that day,
Turning the bitter blade,   barring death's entrance.
The heir of Ecgtheow   would have accepted death,
Under the wide world,   that warrior of Geatland,
Had not that hauberk well-hardened   helped turn the blow
But the blessed God of battles   brought him deliverance,
The high king of Heaven,   the holiest Maker,
The God of goodness   gave him this gift;

Once again, Beowulf is fighting bare-handed.

The great warrior got up,   regaining his stance.

Twenty-Fourth Fitt
Beowulf kills Grendel's mother in her lair

Beowulf sees an ancient sword, one made by the giants (ettins). He tries using that one.

He saw a great sword,   a slasher from old time,
Ancient doom from the ettins,   with an edge well-   1560
  tempered,
A warrior's war treasure,   a weapon unmatched,
Too hard and heavy   to be held by three men
To brandish in battle,   in the brunt of war.
It had been forged by fell giants,   fashioned to cut.
Our Shielding held that hilt,   and hit and struck with
  it,
Emboldened with battle-lust,   that blow was great;
He was wrathful and reckless,   his rage was just.
It pierced her proud her neck,   the point went deep,
Her spine snapped;   the blade sliced clean through
Her blotched body,   blood went to the floor with her.   1570
His blade was blood-wet,   his boast erupted.
Then light lifted the darkness   and luminous was the
  cave,
As when from high heaven   there is heat and light
From God's good candle.   The great hall he looked
  over.
He went by the wall,   his weapon held high,
Hygelac's thane held it,   hoisted in victory,
Still angry, still furious.   That sharp edge was useful
To that wise warrior now.   He wanted quick restitution
From Grendel, that grim one,   for his ghoulish raids,
On the West-Danes in war,   in his wicked hate,   1580
More frequently feuding,   far more than just once,

When from Hrothgar's hearth-mates   he held, and he gripped,
In their sleep he slew them,   in slumber they all died.
Fifteen others he fisted,   and furiously bore them off,
Doomed men of the Danes,   to death he carried them,
A hateful, horrible catch.   Our high prince paid him back,
For stone-cold, stretched out,   the silent Grendel lay,
Dealt justice by death,   and done with his feuds,
Tested in battle, taken from life,   with a torn-off arm
1590 In that brave battle at Heorot.   That body suffered much,
When desolate in death   it endured the last strike.
Beowulf bent over,   and the blow severed the head.
Above, wise men waited,   watching the surface,
Holding watch with Hrothgar,   hating the delay.
The tumbling water tossed,   turbid and cloudy,
Blood floated in that bog.   The brave counselors knew,
nodding their gray and good heads,   that a great man was gone.
The warrior would not return;   they waited in vain.
No return in triumph,   no tale of victory
1600 Would be brought   from that battle to their king—
The she-wolf of the sea   successfully sought out his life.
A nagging wait, the ninth hour came.   So noble Shieldings,
Bereaved, left the bluffs;   back homeward they went.
The gold-friend of good men left.   But the Geats remained,
Staring at the surging blood,   sick in their grief,
Their futile wish, their fruitless thought . . .   their friend to see again

After killing Grendel's mother and hacking off Grendel's head, the ancient sword begins to melt.

Below, that blade   began to melt,
In the blood of the battle,   a bitter thaw,
A weapon of war   went like ice in the springtime;
All of it like ice,   every bit of it melted—   *1610*
Like water ropes unwound   when the Father unties them,
Looses the fetters of frost,   and frees up the water,
Ruling times and tempests—   the true God forever!
The Weder warrior   would take nothing away,
Though plenty of precious things   were piled around.
He gripped Grendel's head   and the great hilt of the sword,
Bedizened and dazzling.   The dark blood melted the sword,
Burned up the blade   with her blood hot with malice,
The poisonous and polluted blood   of she who perished there.
Soon that great swimmer,   who struggled to victory,   *1620*
Who bested two demons in battle,   breasted and kicked his way up.
The currents were cleared,   the sea creature was gone,
From that watery waste,   since the wandering ghoul
Left this life,   lost to this world.
He then swam to the shore,   that sailor-protector,
Solid in soul,   in the spoil rejoicing,
Holding that head,   and the hilt of the sword.
The Geats greeted him gladly   as God they all thanked,
That band of brave warriors,   who believed him now,
Seeing him safe   and sound in return.   *1630*
Soon that hero's helmet   and heavy mail shirt
Were taken as the tale was told.   The bog returned,

Subsiding to silence,   the stain of blood still there.

Lighthearted they left,   looking to the paths back,
High in their hearts,   their heads held high,
As they reckoned the road.   Real men
Carried that craggy head   from the cliff at the shore,
A strain for strong men,   a solid haul,
A feat for the faithful,   since four men carried it
1640 Placed on pole,   impaled on a spear,
To get Grendel's great head   to the gold-hall of Heorot.
So marching in their might,   these men of valor came
To the hall-doors of Heorot,   high-hearted Geats,
In formation as for fighting.   Their feudal lord
Marched with these men,   across meadows in pride.
Then that warrior walked in,   welcome to the hall,
Fearless and famed,   a fighter in truth,
A hard man, head high,   and Hrothgar was greeted.
Grendel's head was hauled,   by the hair it was hauled
1650 Into the hall where heroes sit.   Grendel's head was dragged,
A marvelous sight to men of birth,   a marvel to the queen,
A shocking sight;   they stared in awe.

Reading 7
Questions

Make sure you double-check your answers in the back of the book.

1. Beowulf's statement about revenge (lines 1386–1391) is interesting, given what the poet has just finished telling us in the Finnsburg Episode. We know what Beowulf thinks about revenge, but what does the poet think? Does he agree with Beowulf? Why or why not?

2. Why do you think that Beowulf would ask Hrothgar to take care of his men if he dies? Why wouldn't they just go home?

3. There's some interesting stuff going on with the swords in the battle with Grendel and with Grendel's mother. What do you notice?

4. Do you notice anything Tolkien is borrowing from Anglo-Saxon culture? Make a note of anything you see.

Twenty-fifth Fitt
Beowulf recounts story, hilt

    Beowulf broke out,   that brave son of Ecgtheow,
    "See this sundered head,   son of Halfdane,
    Lord and leader of Shieldings,   we love what we've brought,
    These tokens of triumph;   take it all in.
    I strove in my spirit,   saving my life
    Through warfare in water,   a great work was done
    In struggle and strain,   my strength was waning,
1660   My fight was failing,   faltering . . . had the Lord not saved me.
    I held in both hands   Hrunting the sword
    And that weapon of war   is worthy and good,
    But the Ruler of all realms   gave a reckoning kindness
    When I saw a sword hanging   in splendor and brightness,
    Gigantic and good—   God guided me to it,
    A friend to the friendless—   so I fought with it,
    Felling those fearsome ones,   fate was behind me,
    Slaying with that sword   the sentries both there.
    The blade burned up   when the blood touched it
1670   In the heat of hot battle;   the hilt is here with me
    From my enemies, adversaries.   I avenged their wickedness,
    The death of good Danes,   due as straight justice.
    I can tell you truly   that we've taken Heorot back,
    Now safe to sleep in   with your soldiers and thanes,

Beowulf is careful to be complimentary about Unferth's sword, which is a bit odd.

All your people, all your folk,   everyone from the tribe,
Whether young or old;   no aching fear,
Lord and leader of Shieldings,   will leap from that darkness again,
Dealing dark death   that you dared not confront."
Then the great gold hilt   was given to the gray-beard king,
Placed in the hand of the hero,   who held it in joy.   *1680*
Giant smiths sought to forge it,   they summoned their craft.
After the downfall of demons,   the Danish lord took it,
The work of wise smith-craft,   the world being free
Of that grotesque ghoul,   God's mortal foe,
Murdering monster,   and his mother with him.
It passed into possession   of the people's great lord,
The best king between   all boundaries of the seas,
Who gave out his gold,   good gifts through Scandinavia.
Hrothgar held forth—   with the hilt in his hand,
That ancient heirloom of old,   with etchings and runes   *1690*
From the day of great doom   when a devastating flood,
A wall of great waves   wiped out the giants.
Their fight was futile,   their fate was determined,
Strangers to God, sunk in their sin,   scores were settled by God,
When with a rush the Ruler   wrecked them with water.
On the hilt of that heavy gold,   on the handgrip from old times,
Were runes wisely written,   and the runes described
For whom the snake-bladed sword   was singly wrought,
The best of all blades   from bygone days,
That Titans' hilt well entwined.   The tall king spoke,   *1700*

Turns out that this isn't just a giant sword—it's a giant sword from before the flood.

The high-hearted son of Halfdane.   The hall was silent—
"Now I tell the truth,   the tale may be told,
A man mindful of truth   may say in all honesty,
That this man is mighty,   and his marvelous strength
Belongs to the best,   who battles have won.
Your fame, my great friend,   will go farther than all.
Beowulf the brave   will be the boast of all nations.
You will keep your signal strength   with simplicity of wisdom.
My love, a king's constant,   will keep you, sustain you.
1710 In coming years, when danger creeps,   you will keep your people,
A hero to help them.   Heremod was not that way,
The heir of Ecgwela,   the Honor-Shieldings' lord,
Who did not grow great for their good,   but for gruesome killing,
Death for Danes,   doom from their own king.
Heart-swollen, hateful,   his own hall filled with blood,
Killing table companions!   So that king passed alone,
Exiled for his anger,   excluded from gladness.
Though that man was mighty,   by his Maker endowed,
Given power and purpose,   yet pride crept in.
1720 Though favored and fortunate,   he was fierce in his greed.
His heart-hoard expanded,   and he hardly gave rings
To the Danes as their due;   he died as he lived, joyless,
After suffering and straining,   after struggling for nothing,
To hurt his own hall.   Here is the lesson—
Let virtue lead you.   This life teaches much,
For those wise from many winters.   The wonder is

Hrothgar can tell that Beowulf will be a king someday, and he gives him some advice on being a good king, not like Heremod.

Heremod ended by killing his own thanes. The beginning of his downfall was pride.

> great—
> How God Almighty is good,   giving grace to men,
> How His Spirit gives strength   in the sending of wisdom,
> Wealth, or wide holdings.   He wields all things.
> The Ruler of all realms   gives riches to some,   *1730*
> Lets a high-hearted hero   hold onto adventures,
> Gives him holdings and halls,   and high thrones in them.
> Strongholds, sure fortresses   are secure in his hand,
> Treasures, great tracts of land,   and towers are his,
> A valiant kingdom so vast   that the vanity is invisible,
> And a lackwit with no wisdom   cannot weather a crisis.
> So he rules from feast to feast,   with fate slowly stalking him,
> No sickness, no sadness,   no shadows to trouble him,
> No malevolent malice   mars his banquets,
> No swords are sharpened,   no soldiers muster against him.   *1740*
> The world hears his will,   and willingly follows him,

Twenty-Sixth Fitt
Hrothgar admonishes and retires

> Until concealed pride is conceived   and contrives to grow,
> Wakens and widens,   while the watchman sleeps on,
> That sentry of the soul.   His sleep is too deep,
> And masters his mind;   the murderer creeps closely,
> In evil his arrows   are aimed with his bow.
> He is hit, although helmeted,   his heart is pierced,

Hrothgar warns Beowulf that when God gives riches and blessings, it's easy to become complacent. And when the sentry of the soul falls asleep, pride can slip in and wreak havoc in the heart. This imagery of a night marauder should be familiar to us now.

A shaft shatters him;   no shelter available,
From the wicked little whispers   of this worm-tongued fiend.
1750 What he long held as luxury   seems little to him now,
Greedy for gold,   he gives no more rings,
Savage and sullen,   the summoning fate
He doubts and despises,   and the debt God gave him,
That Worker of wonders,   giving wealth, fame, and glory.
But the end arrived,   the entrance of doom,
When the frail frame of the body   in fragility surrendered,
Fated to fall,   and fearless raiders come
To pillage and plunder   the proud king's old jewels,
The riches of royalty,   the ruins of pride.
1760 So Beowulf, friend, ban such thoughts.   Better be humble,
As the best of brave men,   the better part take;
Eternal gains, everlasting life.   Arrogance is death,
Famed warrior and friend.   The flower of your youth
Was strength sustained,   but soon it will be
That sickness or sword stroke   will slice it clean from you,
Or the flickering flames,   or a flood swelling banks,
Or a blade's bitter slash,   or the brunt of a spear,
Or loathsome old age;   or your eyes start to go,
Dimming in darkness.   Death is surefooted
1770 And will run to this reckoning,   though the runes are heroic.
Without faltering, for fifty long years   I furnished the Danes

Once pride has come in, what was once a blessing is now not enough and greed is the inevitable result.

Hrothgar remembers how he was strong, rich, complacent, and then Grendel came and ruined everything.

With wealth through great warfare,　and warded off foes,
Many and mighty　from middle-earth over,
By sword and spear,　by strength and main,
No foe was formidable enough　to fight under the sun.
But fate twisted and turned on me,　night terror beset us,
Grief came to grind us　when Grendel arose
To harrow this hall,　a hellish enemy.
Those raids nigh ruined us,　unresting, tormented,
Heavy and heart-sick.　But Heaven is good, *1780*
The eternal and everlasting God　extended our lives,
That I after this evil　have eyes that can rest
On this hilt and that head,　cut hard from his shoulders!
Join your comrades in joy,　jubilant, triumphant,
A warrior of worth!　Wealth will come in a torrent
When day dawns,　and your due shall be yours."
The Geat prince was glad　and gained his honors,
He sought out his seat　as the sage king required.
Then again, as before gathered,　these good men all feasted,
Their courage contained,　coiled and ready, *1790*
High-hearted in the hall.　The helmet of night came,
Dusk then deepened.　Those daring ones rose,
So the grizzled and gray-headed　would go to their rest,
The strong Shielding　and the splendid Geat,
Though sturdy and strong　for sleeping longed.
He was a furious fighter,　a famed wanderer
From far away,　so a favored courtier led them,
Who with pride and polish　provided courtly care,

  Such as told well with travelers when they tired of the road,
1800 Or of the swan-road, the sea, when spent with their journey
  That great guest slept under the gables of gold,
  And his sleep was sound; safety reigned in the hall.
  Until bright calls from the blackbird gave the best of the morning,
  With a splendid sunrise. Light spread everywhere,
  Shining followed shadows. The shield-Geats hurried;
  Those earls were eager to exit homeward,
  To get back to blessed hearth, and their bold warrior leader
  Wished to steer his ship toward their summoning homes.
  Beowulf had brought back the blade called Hrunting
1810 To Unferth son of Ecglaf, and urged him to take it,
  That splendid sword, and swore he was thankful;
  He considered it a keen blade, constant in battle.
  Its weakness in warfare he would not mention,
  How the iron edge failed, an empty try—a high-hearted man.
  Impatient for parting, present in armor,
  The warriors were waiting, while he went to the king,
  That throne dear to the Danes. The daring warrior
  Came to the high-seat of Hrothgar and haled him warmly.

They spend their first uninterrupted night in the hall.

Again Beowulf is careful to compliment Hrunting and doesn't hurt Unferth's feelings by telling him it didn't work.

Twenty-Seventh Fitt
Beowulf's farewell, gifts referred to

  Bold Beowulf spoke, brave son of Ecgtheow—

"We seafaring sailors   would now say our desire,   *1820*
To return from this trip   and treasure bring to Hygelac.
Here in this hall   we found a host well-suited;
Well-treated, taken care of,   our tale will praise you.
If by fighting my fealty   can fasten more strongly
So that your love, great lord,   will lift ever higher
Than I have done through my deeds   in desperate adventures,
Know I am willing for war,   still willing to fight.
If I should hear, across the high seas,   that hostile neighbors
Have attacked and assaulted   to engage you in battle.
As they have persecuted in the past,   to place their feet   *1830*
in your hall . . .
Thousands of thanes   I thence shall bring,
Great heroes to help you.   Hygelac will help,
Guardian prince of his people,   he will press to your aid,
Though in truth he is tender,   he will tell with his bravery
By both word and battle,   that bold I might serve you,
Bringing weapons of war   to win you the victory,
Fresh troops to your trial,   from our tested alliance.
If Hrethric visits Hygelac,   the hall of the Geats,
He can count on our king,   and a court full of friends.
A victor should visit   adventuresome lands,   *1840*
Many men will be mindful   of a man who is strong."
Hrothgar answered him,   holding forth like a king,
"These good words are God's,   He gave them to you,
Heaven-sent to your soul!   Such sagacious counsel
From a seer so young,   so strong in mind and body.
That greatness in a grasp,   and good with your mind,

Beowulf says that Hrothgar's son is welcome to visit anytime.

> # BEOWULF: READING 8

You are wise with words.   I wonder not
If Hrethel's heir should die,   hurt fatally in battle,
By spear, or sword,   or struck some other way,
1850 By illness or empty herbs,   and your elder and prince should die,
And he rests, returning to dust,   and life remains for you—
There is no better choice as chieftain   chosen from the Sea-Geats,
Than you, despite youth,   than you for their king.
The Geats—a hoard-guard of heroes,   if you held the throne,
Lord over your own land.   Your life pleases me
The more I meditate on it,   the more I know you, Beowulf!
You have brought a bond   for both our peoples,
For sons of Geats, sons of Danes,   spearmen both,
Shall now pursue peace,   and pull away from strife,
1860 And the wars we once waged,   as our warriors learn restraint.
A long as I live,   as long as I rule here,
Let us take our turns   as treasure is exchanged,
As we greet each other with gifts   across the gannet's-bath and home,
And the ring-prowed riders   bear ring proud givers,
With tokens of our trust.   I take it in faith
That our friends and foes   will be faced together
As we hold in honor   the health of the ancient ways."
So in the hall of Halfdane's heir   Hrothgar offered riches,
Twelve great treasures,   and told him farewell,
1870 Bidding him to bear them home   to his beloved land,

Hrothgar is very impressed with Beowulf's wisdom and predicts that Beowulf will end up as king of the Geats.

To sail home safely,   and soon to return.
Then the kindly king   kissed him warmly,
The Shieldings' sovereign   in sorrow embraced him,
Took his neck and held tight.   The tears flowed
From the great and gray-headed king,   the good Hrothgar.
He held to this hope,   though heavy with winters,
That God would give him   a greeting chance once more,
To hear this Geat in his hall.   This hero was dear to him.
His chest was tight, a tempest there   brought tears from the deep,
His sorrow of soul   had a secret hall,   1880
Bound in breast,   for that beloved man
Burned in his blood.   Then Beowulf departed,
Glorious in gold,   the grass under his feet,
His gestures rejoicing.   His good ship waited,
Kept by the cold anchor,   its captain awaiting.
They bent their way toward the beach,   they blessed Hrothgar's gifts,
They praised him repeatedly.   He was a prince without peer,
Beloved and blameless,   until broken by years,
His splendid strength taken,   as years spare no man.

Reading 8
Questions

Make sure you double-check your answers in the back of the book.

1. What is the example of Heremod meant to illustrate? How does that tie in with the theme of treasure? Hrothgar tells Beowulf to guard his soul against what? What imagery does Hrothgar use in his exhortation? What should that remind us of?

2. Do you notice anything Tolkien is borrowing from Anglo-Saxon culture? Make a note of anything you see.

Twenty-eighth Fitt
Beowulf sails, bad queen, Geatland refurbished

1890   These warriors came wending   their way to the coast,
Brave-hearted and bold,   bearing their armor,
Links of battle metal, burnished   bright in their triumph,
The coast-guard courageous   kept them in view,
From the brow of the bluff   no boasting taunts came,
Or reached the riders   as the guard rode to meet them.
He welcomed the warriors,   those Weders who came,
Bright-armored brave fighters,   believing in joy.
The ship on the strand   was seaworthy and wide,
Laden with riches, ring-prowed,   riding at anchor.
1900   The tall-masted treasure ship,   to take the wealth homeward,
Rose high over the hoard gold   that Hrothgar had given.
Beowulf gave their boat-guard   a blade bound in gold,
A present of pride   on the plank in the mead-hall,
He was esteemed and honored,   that ancient blade with him.
Then their keel carved water,   they caught the wind
And drove the deep water   with Denmark behind them.
They hoisted high the wind-coat   and held it with ropes
Tight to the tall mast;   their timbers creaked.
The wind behind worked them,   that wave-skimmer

flew,
Steady and sure,   speeding toward home,   *1910*
Foam-throated she flew,   fleet like an arrow.
Her bow cut the currents,   and kept her on course,
Till coming they caught sight   of the cliffs of the Geats,
The headlands of home.   Hard the boat drove,
Brought by blustering winds   to the beach proudly.
The harbor-guard held watch,   holding hope for return,
Waiting long for loved warriors   who had left for Denmark.
By the water he waited   and watched a long time.
The ship, broad in the beam,   was bound to the shore,
With the right anchor-ropes,   resisting the surf,   *1920*
Lest those long-trusted timbers   should tear themselves loose.
Then Beowulf beckoned,   "Bear this treasure ashore."
There were gems, and gold,   and goodly amounts more.

An interesting sidenote: Hygelac's name means "without wisdom," but his wife is named Hygd, which means "wisdom." Seems like an unfortunate combination of names.

Hygd is a good queen—not like this other one that we're about to hear about.

That were gifts all to go   to the giver of rings,
Hygelac, son of Hrethel,   in his hall by the sea,
Close to the cliffed sea-wall,   a kingly estate.
That hall was high,   his haven was splendid,
A majestic king, magnificent,   his queen marvelous,
Hygd was wise and well-spoken,   though her winters were few
In that formidable fortress   where she found herself.   *1930*
Haereth's high-hearted daughter,   she held to high standards
And gave out great gifts   to the Geats of their court.
Thryth's pride was not present in her,   Hygd prevailed with kindness,

Unlike that cruel queen   who with crimes held sway.
Though dauntless, none dared look on her,   however
  deep his courage.
Only her lord, he alone,   of all the men at court
Could look on that lady   her likeness to see.
Fetters would fasten him   and find his doomed
  madness,
A black and dark bondage.   A brief wait passed
1940 And a burnished blade   brought an end to his life,
The penalty pronounced   to the people assembled.
The custom of queens   should not come to this—
A peace-weaver punishing?   Pursuing blood?
Demanding more wrath,   murdering warriors?
A man's life lost,   left desolate for nothing?
But Hemming's high kinsman   held back her ways.
Ale drinkers agreed   and also told tales;
Her outrages, her onslaughts,   her eager cruelties
Were made less, diminished,   when she made her
  journey,
1950 Going as bride gold-bedecked   to a good hero and
  prince,
A high and haughty noble   in the hall of Offa.
Over the foaming flood   at her father's wish,
She sought her new home safely,   and since then
  flourished
In great royal riches   and a regal throne,
Fitted by fate   for the fame she was given,
She loved long and hard   that lord of warriors.
Of all the high heroes   he was honored the most,
From sea to sea,   excelling all others.
Presented with praise   for his power in war,
1960 Offa fought fiercely   freeing his homeland.

After a bad start, Thryth's marriage to Offa seems to have calmed her down.

That warrior worked as a king,   wisely he reigned
Over the extent of his kingdom.   Eomer his son
Was a help of heroes   and Hemming's kinsman,
Grandson of Garmund   and great in warfare.

Twenty-Ninth Fitt
Hygelac receives Beowulf, Freawaru warning

Beowulf crossed the beach,   his best warriors with him,
The wide sea-strand   was silently waiting for them.
The world-candle warmed them,   wending its southern course.
With sturdy gait they strode,   they strode along
To the place their prince waited,   to their protector they went,
Where the brave young battle-king   in his beautiful hall,   *1970*
King truly, keeper and giver of rings,   killer of Ongentheow,
In his fortress for fighters.   To famous Hygelac
Beowulf's return was told,   the tale ran ahead—
There in the king's court   where kinsmen take refuge,
His shield-friend was safe,   both sound and alive,
And he walked, well and joyful,   welcomed through the yards.
The high king of the hall   ordered hasty preparations,
And space for these strong ones   was soon made ready.
He sat by his sovereign,   returned safe from adventure,
Kinsman with kin.   His kingly lord   *1980*
Had greeted him graciously,   and given him welcome
With earnest, ordered formal words.   The ale was flowing

When Haereth's high-hearted daughter   through the
   hall entered.
She was a friend to fighters,   and filled up their cups,
Held up by those heroes.   Hygelac then asked
His comrade questions   and kept on asking—
In the high-beamed hall—   hungry to know
Their adventures, their odyssey,   how eager for battle
   they were.
"What came of your call,   my kinsman Beowulf,

1990 When you jumped to the journey   to join with the
   Danes
Over the salty sea,   seeking to do battle,
Hellish warfare in Heorot?   Could you help their
   king,
Lift the grief of their great chief,   give aid to Hrothgar
In his well-known woe?   Waves of sorrow
Surged in my sadness;   I saw disaster coming
To my good friend's greatness,   I gave many requests
That you not go to grapple   with Grendel's bloody
   claws,
But to cede to the South-Danes   the settlement of that
   fight,
Let them give battle to Grendel!   But God be thanked,

2000 For your safe return, sound,   and sitting beside me."
Then brave Beowulf spoke,   the best son of
   Ecgtheow,
"O Hygelac, what happened   is hardly obscure,
Many men have heard it,   that mashed meeting we
   had,
That great and grim battle   between Grendel and me,
Which we held in the hall   where his hatred would
   vent

When he slaughtered Shielding-Victors,   sending them grief,
Misery after misery.   I made all that right.
No spawn of that sin-creature   can spin out a boast,
None that now live,   for that night war before dawn,
Can boast of that battle,   for beaten were they,   2010
As I fought that vile flesh.   But first was an audience,
I went to Hrothgar's great hall,   to hale that ring-giver,
Halfdane's high kinsman,   on his hall-throne victorious.
As soon as he saw   that I sought out this purpose,
He soon seated me   with his son and his heir.
As I love this good life—   his lieutenants were valiant,
Such mead made from honey   and merry laughter.
I have not heard under heaven!   His high-hearted queen,
Wealhtheow, peace-weaver,   wove through the hall,
Encouraged the kinsmen,   and gave clasps and rings.   2020
She then sought out her seat   and summoned more gifts.
Hrothgar's daughter, dark beauty,   would dance through the rows,
Offering ale,   to earls in their turn.
Her name was known to us,   not obscure to hall-warriors.
Freawaru was that fitting name,   as the fine gold cup
She extended and offered.   Engaged she was,
That gold-decked damsel,   to the dauntless son of Froda.
The Shielding-king sought this,   as it seemed wise to him,
To keep safe his kingdom;   he considered it prudent

Freawaru is the daughter of Hrothgar. We are told here that she was engaged to be married as a peaceweaver. Beowulf gives his candid opinion of how well that's going to work out. But remember back in line 85 (in the foreshadowing about the future of Heorot) we are told that the end comes through a son-in-law.

2030   To make fast a marriage   and master the feuds,
       Stop the slaughtering.   But seldom it happens,
       When someone was slain,   that the spears may rest,
       Though the bride be beautiful,   but a brief time.
       "The Heathobards may hate it,   at the hall wedding feast,
       When Ingeld enters,   his arm offered to that woman.
       And the Danes, dauntless all,   dared to bring heirlooms,
       Escorting the eager peace-weaver   from the entrance to their seats,
       And on their hips are those heirlooms,   old Heathobard treasures,
       Hilted and hard,   high treasures, ring-decked,
2040   Weapons of war   that they wielded at one time
       Until they lost their linden-shields,   and lives not a few,
       On the fields of fighting,   with their final losses.

At one time the Danes had conquered the Heathobards, and now they're carrying Heathobard swords which they won in battle.

Thirtieth Fitt
Story of Ingeld

       Then some old captain in his cups   will catch a glimpse
       Of an ancient heirloom,   and, being old, he remembers
       The spear-death of his soldiers—   he smolders in anger—
       His cold heart turns cruel,   he catches a young eye
       And tries his temper,   tests his resolve.
       He awakens old wars   with whispering words:
       "Comrade, can you not see?   Did you catch that sword's glint?
2050   That was the weapon   which your father carried

Beowulf is speculating about what will happen at the wedding when the Heathobards start to recognize those swords—their father's swords—on the hips of their old enemies.

To his final fight   in that feud from old times,
That bravest of blades,   when the battle-Danes took him,
When Wethergeld fell in war   and the waste of that loss
Was our heroes' hurt   at the hands of the Shieldings?
So here is the son   of that swaggering Dane,
Proud in his pacing,   presumptuous in conceit,
He rejoices in your jealousy,   and that jeweled hilt carries
On his hateful hip,   that blade should be held,
rightfully, by you."
So he aggravates and urges   and eggs on that warrior
With sharp and shrewd words   till the shameful moment   *2060*
When Freawaru's fallen thane,   for his father's war deed,
Is battered in blood   and a blade split him open,
His life entirely lost.   The lieutenant assassin flees.
He knows that cold country   and can find secret paths.
Peace is broken on both sides,   and battle looms,
Their oaths are not owned   when Ingeld's breast heats up
Filling with fury,   wanting to fight, not love,
And his care for his peace-queen   grow cooler and wanes.
So why hold up high   the Heathobards' faith,
Their debt to the Danes,   or their enduring trust   *2070*
And purchase of peace?   But let us pass on from this,
Turning again to Grendel,   that you may grasp the story,
O royal ring-giver,   and the results of that fight,
That hand battle with hell.   When heaven's jewel
Had crossed the clear sky,   that cruel monster came,

Beowulf doesn't think this marriage will go well.

That dread bringer of death,   to deal out his malice
Where still sound enough   we set our watch for the hall.
That hater seized Hondscio,   with his hands tore him up,
He was fated to fall.   He was first to die;
2080 Grendel gobbled him,   that belt-girded warrior,
Our good and gracious thane   was gripped in death,
And that brave man's body   was bolted down.
Yet Grendel wouldn't go   from that golden hall,
Eagerly chewing entrails   but still empty-handed.
His mind was full of murder,   and his maw with bloody teeth,
So he grabbed me greedily   and got as good as he gave,
Though his presence was powerful.   A pouch hung by his side,
Cunningly made with clasps,   and kept tight with bands,
A wondrous work devised,   in black wisdom wrought,
2090 By dark and devilish arts   from dragon pelts.
He thought to throw me in,   though an innocent man,
That fatal loathsome fiend   would fight to thrust me in
With many other men.   He might have prevailed
Had I not suddenly stood   to strike him back in anger.
My tale would take too long   if I told the whole story,
How I paid that predator back;   a grave penalty for his deeds.
But I proved in that place,   dear prince, your people's honor,
My fighting gained fame.   His flight clattered out
To a little more life,   the less the better.
2100 But the wreck of his right arm   remained in the hall,

Here we are given some details that we didn't hear the first time around, like Grendel's bag made of dragon skin which he wanted to put Beowulf into.

Held by us in Heorot.   That hellish one fled
To die in the darkness   on the deep ocean floor.
The Shielding friend said   that the struggle was worth
The gifts he would give,   gold in plenty,
Treasure untold,   when the tall dawn came,
And we gratefully gathered   in the great mead-hall.
There were stories, then songs,   and a Shielding,
   gray-headed,

Beowulf remembers how Hrothgar told stories of his youth and his great battles—an old king, looking back on his life.

Battle tested, battle tried,   told of the old times.
Then suddenly some hero   would sing with his harp,
His chanting-word chosen   to sing cheerful lays,   2110
With sad songs as well,   all settled in truth,
Amazing and marvelous.   The majestic king
Told tales from his youth,   told of times long past,
When he could strike with strength,   but now
   struggled with age,
A gray-headed great one;   his good heart ached
As his mind mulled over   those melted battle marvels.
So in the hall of Heorot,   the whole of that day,
We talked and we tasted   until the night fell.
Grendel's mother mauled us,   another murder to deal
   with.
She sought victory in vengeance,   vile in malice;   2120
Her son was slain,   she sought his killers,
Got revenge on the Geats.   Grendel's mother
   monstrous
Fell in a fury   and fought with us there,
Avenged her son on Aeschere,   attacked that good
   counselor,
That loyal thane lost his life,   his light was gone.
When the morning mist came,   our mourning was
   broken,

When the Danes could not deal   with this death by
  their custom—
His body could not be burned,   that best warrior
  advisor,
Away under the water,   wailing and cackling,
2130 She carried that corpse   in the clutch of a fiend.
Hrothgar, heavy-hearted,   was hurt beyond speaking.
That burden almost broke him,   that brave lord of his
  people.
That great prince implored me,   pleaded with anguish,
To seek the sea's bottom   and summon up vengeance,
To brave that beast's power,   take battle down to her.
For goodness and glory   and great honor with men.
He would richly reward me.   I resolved to fight, it is
  known,
And found that fierce monster   on the floor of the sea.
The hand-battle was hard,   her foul hall was the place
2140 Where blood soaked the brine   and bespattered the
  walls.
With a high-hilted blade   I took her head off,
From Grendel's grotesque mother,   and gained my own
  life,
I barely bested her—   my brave end was not yet.
Then Halfdane's son, Hrothgar,   that helper of
  warriors,
Gave great gifts to me,   both gear and fine riches.

Reading 9
Questions

Make sure you double-check your answers in the back of the book.

1. In this section we hear Beowulf's assesment of the peaceweaver success rate. What is the poet (through Beowulf) saying?

2. Do you notice anything Tolkien is borrowing from Anglo-Saxon culture? Make a note of anything you see.

Thirty-first Fitt
Beowulf loyal to Hygelac, becomes king of the Geats

"So this king kept faith,   the customs of old,
And I lacked for little.   No lesser gifts were offered
The recompense and reward   was righteous—true gifts
From Halfdane's heir,   which I have from him.
2150   Now to you, my prince and pride,   I present them all,
I give them all gladly.   Your goodness alone
Is my favor and fealty.   Few others I have
As kinsmen this close,   except, kind Hygelac, you."
The boar-head standard brought,   Beowulf presented it,
And a high helmet for war,   and a hauberk gray,
A sword of splendor,   then speaking he said—
"This weaponry and war-gear   was wisely given
By Hrothgar, that hero,   and holding it out,
He said that its story   should straightway be told you—
2160   King Heregar held it,   heroic in battle,
Lord for a long time,   in the land of the Shieldings,
Did not bequeath this corselet   with the crown to his son,
That is, Hereward, dauntless and daring,   as dear as he was.
This best battle-harness—   may blessings attend it!"
I then heard that four horses   in harness and valiant,
Dappled and daring,   decked out in trappings,
Each one like the others,   eager for battle,
He gave his good prince.   So great-hearted kinsmen

Should not weave with wiles,   or work in craftiness,
Or with deep deceptiveness   bring death out of hiding.   2170
This nephew and neighbor   was never treacherous
To Hygelac the high-hearted,   holding him dear.
Both of them believed in   what was best for the other.
I heard, too, of the torque,   a treasure for Hygd,
A wonderful gift, wrought gold,   which Wealhtheow gave to him,
A mild daughter of majesty—   three mettlesome steeds also,
High-stepping horses,   with hand-wrought leather saddles.
Bright on her breast   was that bright torque of the queen's.
The son of Ecgtheow showed   his settled heart,
As a man known for nobility,   and not for malice.   2180
High honor was his;   In the hall of ale he would not
Kill his comrades,   free from cruelty in heart,
Although among men,   his might was the greatest,
A gift from God,   that glorious strength,
Above all brave warriors.   Belittled a long time
As worthless by warriors,   as weak by the Geats.
His prince wouldn't pick him,   his power unseen,
His favor failed him   in the feasting hall.
Slothful and slack   the stronger men thought him,
A prince far too passive,   no promise at all.   2190
But real change was chosen   when the chance arose.
Then the brave bulwark king   bade them bring a treasure,
Hrethel's heirloom,   hilt covered with gold,
A blade embellished,   no better anywhere,
A treasure in truth,   a trust with the Geats.

    That bright blade was laid   on Beowulf's knees,
    And holdings from Hygelac,   measured in hides, seven thousand,
    With a hall and high seat.   These holdings were common,
    But the birthright of both   was best for the king,
2200 Because his rule in the realm   was right and unquestioned,
    Until the Geat king gave it   as a good gift of honor.
    Now it was left to him later   by the levying years,
    Proud Hygelac perished   through the penalty of war,   *Skipping ahead:*
    And Heardred with Hygelac,   by the hard blades of battle,   *Hygelac dies.*
    Under the sheltering shield-wall   that slaughter left them,
    When the fighting Swedish foe   found them defending
    The good Geat townships   with great courage.
    They hunted Hereric's nephew   and hurt him in battle.
    So Beowulf the brave   a broad realm came to rule,   *Beowulf takes*
2210 As defender for fifty winters,   and was found to rule well.   *the throne and*
    As head and high prince   he held the throne,   *has ruled for fifty*
    A wise and wizened king   until the worm came,   *years when the*
    A deadly raging dragon   from the depths of night.   *dragon shows up.*
    In the heathery hills   a hidden treasure lay,   *Suddenly Beowulf*
    In a stone cave on a craggy slope.   A straight path ran there,   *is in the identical*
    A hidden mountain hold.   But a hurrying man   *position that*
    Came to that cave   and crept inside   *Hrothgar was*
    To that heathenish hoard.   His hand soon found   *at the beginning*
    A cup encrusted with gems,   which he kept as he left.   *of the poem. An*

old king, having ruled fifty years, is suddenly plagued with a monster.

The thief slipped away silently   from the sleeping   2220
  worm,
But soon great sorrow   descended on the villages—
They felt the wrath and the rage   of the rampaging
  dragon.

Thirty-Second Fitt
Dragon is disturbed and advances

That churl did not choose   a chance at the treasure,
He did not want to lay waste   to the ways of his
  people,
But in peril, pursued,   some prince's slave
Had fled from a flogging,   in fear sought out shelter,
Crept into that cave,   quite conscious of sinning.
When he entered, not eagerly,   the awful spectacle
Shook him, seized him,   and sent him reeling,
Yet that fool and fugitive   felt in hand something   2230
And in his frightful flight   his feet took him out,
With the treasure cup taken,   and our last tale with it.
There were many other marvels,   magnificent treasure,
Honored heirlooms   in this earth hall were stored
By some ancient adventurer,   an earl with great
  treasure,
Leaving this legacy   as the last of his race,
Cunningly hidden, craftily stored,   a cave to receive it,
Dark below, deep in the ground.   Death had taken the
  others,
And he alone, last hero,   had hidden the gold,
He alone was left   alive from that tribe,   2240
Mourning his men,   missing them deeply,
While the reward his delight,   that wonderful treasure,

Some unknown man, long ago, the last of his tribe, buried all their remaining treasure and the secret died with him.

Was his bitter-love—briefly.   That burial spot, ready,
Near the shore of the sea,   secure on the headland,
Its location was left secret,   lost to all others,
And he laid lordly treasures,   leaving them there,
The heavy gold heaped   and hidden from view
By that guardian of gold rings.   He gave up few words:
"Now keep it, earth cave,   keep it far from all heroes,
2250 This treasure untold,   and their tales buried with it.
Good men grasped it before,   but war got them finally,
Cruelly taking my kin,   to keep them in death,
To rob them of riches,   and the richness of life.
No liegemen are left,   who loved honor and battle,
No hall-joy, high singing,   no holding our cups,
Bright with mead-blessing.   My brave men are lost.
Their hardened helmets   which held golden sections,
Shall have plates fall apart.   The polishing servants
Who burnished their brightness,   for battle preparing,
2260 Have died, and in death   are done with their labors.
The same with their shields,   the same with their mail,
No resisting the rust   that rots out this armor.
No more mail off to battle   with that marauding
    chieftain,
On the back of that brave one.   No blessed harp
    music,
No songs from the strong wood.   No spiraling hunter,
No hawk through the hall,   No horses champing and
    stamping
In the king's ancient courtyard.   The cruelty of death
Swept these sons of men   down that sorrowful river."
With a mind full of mourning,   he murmured his
    grief,
2270 Alone, the last one,   he took leave of them all,

Later, the dragon found the hoard and slept on it for three hundred years.

He wept day to dusk,   until death's surging tide
Swept over his sorrow.   That serpent and worm
Found the hoard that was hidden,   that heathen gold,
Who, with burning breath,   found the barrow at
   midnight,
Firedrake, flame-snake,   a foul dragon with wings,
Enveloped in vice and fire,   the villages below
Fear that fantastic worm.   It is his fate to seek out
   treasure,
Hidden hoards,   all that heathenish gold,
Which he guards in his guile,   and gets nothing from
   it.
For three hundred thorough winters   that worm   2280
   stayed hidden,
Holding his hoard   in that hall down below,
Poisonous, powerful,   till a purloining slave
Kindled his cruelty,   and took a cup to his master,
As a price for his peace,   approaching his lord,
With the booty for bond.   That barrow was pilfered,
Pardon was promised . . .   with the penalty coming,
A wretched return—   but his ruler still saw
A catch of great cunning,   a cup from the old days.
When the drake was done sleeping,   dark woes were
   kindled.
He sniffed along stones   and slithered outside,   2290
Finding a footprint   of the fellow just gone,
Who had stupidly stepped   by the serpent's great head.
So may the lucky in life   leave disaster behind,
Whether exile or agony,   when the Almighty pleases
To defend them with favor,   though feckless they be.
That guardian of gold   over ground went sniffing
For the miserable man   who made off with that cup.

Aflame with fierce anger   he flew from his barrow,
Cruelty over the crags,   a comfortless land,
2300 No one walked in that wilderness,   yet for warfare he lusted,
And the blood of battle.   The barrow he searched again,
That fine cup to find,   and finally discovered
That some miserable mortal   had man-handled his treasure,
His gems and his gold   that he guarded in malice.
Impatient, petulant,   till past the sundown,
Boiling with black rage   was that barrow drake—
They would pay the penalty,   punished with flame
For dear drinking cup's loss.   Now day was gone
As the drake had desired;   he dove from his wall,
2310 No longer lingering,   but lusting with fire,
Enfolded by flames,   a fright from the skies,
For the residents of that realm,   their ruin soon coming,
And the grief of their good lord,   and his grievous death.

Thirty-Third Fitt
Dragon attacks, Beowulf believes he offended God

Then that beast belching fire,   burst down upon them,
Burning bright homes.   The blazes stood out,
Struck fear in falling spirits.   That fatal monster
Left no living thing,   leaving burnt-out homes.
His fired ferocity   and fighting malice
Was widely witnessed,   how that winged serpent
2320 Hounded and harried   the hearts of the Geats.

A grim giver of grief   to those good people.
At dawn, his hidden hoard   was a haven for him.
His flames of fire   had enfolded the people
In a blaze of burning.   To his barrow he retreated,
His bulwark for battle—   a belief that was empty.
Beowulf was brought   the blunt truth straightway,
Death and danger arrived.   His dear homeland
    threatened,
The best of his buildings   in the burning had melted,
With the great throne of the Geats.   That good king
Was sorrowful and sad,   sunken in spirit.   2330
That wise king worried   that the World Ruler
Brought down righteous wrath   for an old-right
    violated,
Testing and trying the Lord.   His tempted breast with
Black thoughts boiled,   as before had not been.
That fiery drake's flame   had flattened their stronghold;
From the cliffs of the coast,   continuously inland,
From the beach to the bluffs,   but their battling king,
A wise prince of the Weders,   worked out a plan.
A massive metal shield   was made by his instruction,
Entirely of iron—   that earl in wisdom knew   2340
That a wooden war-shield   would be worthless,
So with cunning craft   they cast his marvel,
Lest they lose linden to flame.   The life of that prince
Was soon to suffer   the sorrows of death,
His days diminishing,   and the dragon also,
Though his greed and that gold   had gone long
    together.
The ring-giver reckoned it   a wretched shame
To fight that far-flyer   with a fierce host of men,
A boastful band of men;   battle did not frighten him,

Notice that as the dragon first attacks his kingdom, Beowulf's first response is to gear up and go fight.

2350 The dragon's dread presence   he deemed a small thing,
Its vicious foul vigor   and its violence threatening,
He had seen such things before,   and struggles of war,
Conquest in combat,   the cleansing of Heorot,
That great hall of Hrothgar's,   which his hand had freed,
When his grip had killed Grendel,   and in grappling took out
That fierce and foul clan.   That fighter also did well
In the hard war, hand-fighting,   when Hygelac fell,
When the Geat ruler of right   in the roil of battle,
That high son of Hrethel,   heaved his last breath,
2360 Because of hard sword strokes   slashing in Frisia,
Beaten down by blades.   Beowulf fled that place
Through skill in swimming   and the strength of his arms,
Taking thought for thirty mail coats,   thinking to escape
With those coats to the coast—   so he came to the sea.
No great tale for the tribe of Hetware,   no telling vaunt,
As they came to that contest   and carried the fight to him,
Their bucklers were battered,   and blades lost—
Few of those fighters   found their way back home.
Eager for home, Ecgtheow's son   entered the sea and swam,
2370 Forlorn and lonely,   his land to seek.
There Hygd held an offer   of both hoard and realm,
Rings and a royal-throne—   reason told her
That her son had no strength   to save that great throne
From hostile heathen   after Hygelac's fall.

Here we find out more about Hygelac's death and how Beowulf came to the throne. They were at war in Frisia, and Hygelac was killed.

Beowulf swam home, and Hygd asked him to rule because her son was so young.

Beowulf refused, and helped Hygelac's son as an advisor until he too was killed. It was only when the heir was dead that Beowulf began to rule. We see here that Beowulf has been noble and loyal throughout his life.

But in a blow to the bereaved tribe,   Beowulf would not
Accept the rule or royal sway   over his rightful lord's heir,
Young Heardred, son of Hygelac,   that high-born prince.
He supported his sovereign   and served him in honor,
A true friend with all fealty   and favorable counsel,
Until abler, grown older,   he accepted full governance   2380
Of the warlike Weder-Geats.   The water brought exiles
Seeking his support—   they were sons of Ohthere.
They were rebels against the rule   of the royal Swede king,
A shield of Scylfings,   a sea-king of fame,
A giver of gold,   a great, mighty prince.
So Heardred fell hard,   hospitable prince,
And he perished in pain   from a piercing sword,
From the blow of a blade,   that boy-king of Hygelac.
Ongentheow's only son,   Onela, departed
For hearth and home   after Heardred was killed,   2390
Leaving Beowulf behind,   a brave lord for the Geats,
To give gold, and wise guidance—   a good king that was!

Here we see it again: "A good king that was."

Reading 10
Questions

Make sure you double-check your answers in the back of the book.

1. How long has Beowulf been king when the dragon appears? This is a small detail, so why is it significant? What is the poet leading us to notice?

2. We're given a brief history of how Beowulf became king in the first place. Given the themes of kin-killing and revenge, what is the poet showing us?

3. In line 2391, we once again hear the phrase, "A good king that was." How does this compare to the previous times we've heard this?

4. Do you notice anything Tolkien is borrowing from Anglo-Saxon culture? Make a note of anything you see.

Thirty-fourth Fitt
Beowulf hunts dragon in sorrow and despair

    The death of his dear prince   he desired to avenge,
    And gave a gift to Eadgils,   a group of soldiers,
    Reinforcements for a friend,   to fortify resolve.
    Over the waves, over water,   to Ohthere's son,
    Both warriors and weapons came.   He won his revenge
    When the king was killed   after care-ridden raids.
    So through struggles many   the son of Ecgtheow
2400 Had persevered and passed,   through perils abundant,
    With dauntless daring   until this day arrived
    That destined the deed   of the fire-drake battle.
    With eleven others   the aged lord of Geats
    Stood firm, stirred in his anger,   and sought out the dragon.
    He had heard the whole story,   how the harm had arisen,
    The maiming of men.   That marvelous cup
    Had been brought to Beowulf   and bestowed on him.
    A thirteenth man, the thief,   they had thought to bring along,
    The one who stirred the strife   and started everything,
2410 A cringing captive,   that careworn slave,
    Fearful, but forced,   he found the path up
    To the earth-mound entrance,   and the edge of battle,
    Where breakers dashed the barrow   on the bluff near the sea,
    A sea that was surging.   Inside was the treasure,

The thief is being brought along as a guide.

Of glittering gold-work—   and a glaring dragon,
Fierce and formidable,   filled with gold-lust,
He lurked in his lust.   That lair was forbidding,
No easy entrance   for arms to win.
That heroic high king   on the headland sat down,
And spoke solemn words   to succor his men,   2420
As a Geat-king, gold-giver.   Grim was his heart,
Wavering, but wonderful.   Wyrd was upon him,
And was ready to reach   that righteous man,
Hunt down his hoard soul,   and halve it in two,
His breath from his body.   That bold prince's life
Would no longer linger,   and would be lost from his body.

Beowulf begins to think back on his long life. He seems to know that this is the end.

Beowulf spoke boldy,   that brave son of Ecgtheow—
"I have sought out struggles;   I certainly fought
Through terrible troubles.   I have tales from my youth.
My royal Geat ruler   gave me riches of friendship,   2430
Summoned me when seven,   and sought to raise me.
King Hrethel then had me,   a hall-friend from my father,
Gave me food for the feasting   and the favor of kinship.
My life there, I was not least—   he liked me as well,
No better than his birthright sons,   no less blessed than them either—
Herebald and Hathcyn   and Hygelac my lord.
The eldest untimely died   from an unwitting arrow,

More kin-killing.

A kinsman's cruel mistake,   caused his bier to come early,
When Hathcyn's cursed hand   from the horned bow slipped
And a feathered arrow flew   and friend was lost,   2440

The mark was missed,   but mortal man wasn't,
When a bloody battle shaft   caused brotherly grief.
A fearful arrow flight,   and a fatal sorrow,
Heartache for Hrethel,   and harder still than that,
No payment in blood for the prince's death,   no penalty exacted.
It was as the bitterness borne   by a bent old man
When his son has to swing   on the sorrowful gallows,
Riding high for the ravens.   A wretched end,
With a sorrowful song   for the son left there hanging,
2450 The ravens' repast—   no rescue possible
From an elderly, impotent   and aching old man.
Always alone, every morning,   he enters every day,
Knowing the heir is elsewhere gone,   an empty hall left,
All is desolate, he has no desire   to delve in the future,
Waiting to bequeath his wealth   to a ward newborn,
Now that death's dominion   devastated his house.
Miserable man!   He musters the courage to look
On the lodge of his lost son,   the last place of his happiness,
Bereft now of rejoicing.   The rider now sleeps,
2460 That hero, hidden away in death.   Harps no longer play,
In the courtyards no clear songs,   as the custom once was.

Thirty-Fifth Fitt
Beowulf reminisces, challenges dragon, thanes flee

He greets the gulf in his chamber,   a grief song is lifted,

His loss is too large for him.   Too large also all else,
His hall and his hearth.   So the high king of the
  Weders
Carried heavy care   in his collapsed heart for Herebald,
Wave after wave   of woe unrelenting.
Vengeance was averted   by the voice of conscience—
He could not slay his son,   or say words of harassment
For that foul and fatal mistake,   though he favored
  him no more.
For all the sorrow his soul went through,   that seared   2470
  him through,
He gave up all gladness   and God's light chose.
Buildings and all blessings   he bequeathed to his sons,
As a prosperous prince would do   when passing from
  earth.
There was struggling and strife   between the Swedes
  and Geats
Over wide waterways—   the warfare was constant,
Hardscrabble and hand-to-hand,   after Hrethel had
  died,
For Ongentheow's offspring   were still eager for battle,
Settled on strife   and seeking a fight.
They had no passion for peace,   but pummeled their
  way
In hatred of their hosts   near Hreosnabeorh.   2480
My family and friends   fought a feud for just
  vengeance,
Not for spite nor malice,   as is known by all,
Though one of their warriors   won it with blood;
A bargain of bitterness,   for the boldness of Hathcyn
Proved fatal in that fight   for the first of the Geats.
With morning as herald, I heard   the head of the killer

    struck
    And the clansman was conquered   with a clean stroke.
    When Ongentheow eagerly sought   Eofor in battle.
    That war-helm split wide,   and pale white he fell down,
2490   That wise Scylfing warrior.   The wild hand that struck
    Remembered all death debts   and dealt the blow.
    For the gifts he gave me,   my grip on the sword
    Repaid him in plenty,   with the power I brought.
    I had lordly gifts and lands,   laden with his generosity,
    I had a hearth and hall.   He hardly needed
    Swedish mercenaries or men,   or more help from Spear-Danes,
    Or gift help from the Gifthas   to gather support,
    Or some worse warriors   who need wages to fight!
    I fought in the front   and fiercely delivered,
2500   Standing steadfast,   and so I always fight
    While my blade proves bold   and my bravery lasts
    As it has repeatedly proven—   profoundly loyal—
    Since I dealt out death   and Dayraven died,
    Felled by my fisted might,   that Frankish champion.
    He brought no booty back   to the bold king of the Frisians,
    Whether baubles or breast gems,   or bedazzling gold work.
    Rather, slain in that slaughter,   that standard-bearer fell,
    The pride of princes.   A pointed sword didn't do it,
    But his breast bone was shattered   and broken by hand,
2510   His heart beat halted.   The hilted sword now,
    Hard edge in my hand   over hoard gold will battle."

Bold Beowulf spoke, and his brave words were clear,
His finest and final words: "I have fought many wars
In my younger years— now yearning for honor,
A tested and true defender, triumph I seek,
Doing deeds of great daring, if that dragon of fire
Comes from his cavern as I call him to battle!"
Then that great king greeted his good men for the last time,
That high helmeted warrior hailed each of them there,
With dear words of devotion. "I would dare this weaponless,   2520
No sword for this serpent, if I saw it as humble—
Fighting such a foe with fantastic vows
And a grip on his great throat as with Grendel I prevailed.
But here—burning breath and blasts from his nostrils,
And powerful poison, so prepared I have come
With buckler and breastplate. And I won't back away
One step from my station. I will stand to the end
In our war near the wall, as wyrd may allow,
That master of men. My mind is eager
But I am bound to not boast over this battle-flyer.   2530
Now near this barrow abide in your bold armor,
You high-hearted heroes, and hold yourselves back—
You will see soon enough who suffers the worst of it.
Wait out our warfare. This wasting fight
Is for me to make happen, my mettle to measure,
My might with this monster, my mind to keep strong
With high hearted heroics. Hard battle awaits,
And I will win through to wealth or wake up in heaven,
Killed by that cruel one, your kind king and leader."

Beowulf speaks to each of his men before going in to fight.

He's going to go in alone.

2540 Fierce in his fearsome helmet   that fighting champion stood,
   Trusting in his tested strength,   and his last trial faced.
   With his blade and buckler   he bent low and entered
   Under the craggy cliffs—   no coward that one!
   Soon enough the king saw   smoke from that fire—
   That survivor of sure victories,   and certain in bravery,
   From fields of fighting,   when furious men clashed—
   Along the reach of the rampart,   from the rocky stone arch,
   A brook from that barrow   with burning hot water,
   Above it fire flashing,   forbidding any approach.
2550 To hold ground there was hopeless,   hot harm was waiting,
   Dark pain enduring   from the dragon fire.
   Then Beowulf burst out,   rage blasting in a roar,
   His shout was not shallow,   a sure cry from the Geat leader,
   Sturdy in heart, he stormed,   and struck with his voice,
   His cry was courageous, clear,   beneath cliffs of deep gray.
   The dragon in the deep   heard human danger approach,
   And his rage unwrapped,   erupting in violence,
   No pact of peace here.   That pestilent worm
   Came out of the cave   to conquer a man,
2560 Eager in his anger,   the ancient rocks shook.
   Standing by the stone door,   his sturdy shield raised,
   The bold lord Beowulf   braved the onslaught,
   While that coiled cruelty   with cold courage
   Was flared for the fight.   The fell king
   Drew sword from his scabbard,   summoning bravery,

With that ancient heirloom.   Each of them faced off
With an awesome adversary   in an angered high
    mettle.
Stout, standing fast,   he stopped with his shield up,
That leader and lord,   as the loathsome worm coiled
In serpentine spirals.   The splendid king waited.   2570
Now unwinding in wickedness   the worm darted
    forward,
Fiery and fierce.   The firm shield held fast,
Body and soul safely,   but not so long
As the desire of the dauntless one   decided was needed.
The respite he required   was rejected
In his warfare this once.   So wyrd would not have it,
While the high prince held firm   and hewed with his
    blade,
The lord and leader of Geats,   that loathsome foe
    struck
With his ancient heirloom,   but that edge turned
    aside—

The sword doesn't pierce the dragon but it does make him mad.

The bone bent the blade,   and his blow was feebler   2580
Than that high-hearted hero   had need of then,
Harassed and harried as he was.   Then the hoard
    monster
Swelled in riotous rage   in wrath for that blow,
Firing his flames,   fierce in his anger.
Victory was a vain hope;   the vicious breath flared,
And the Weder-lord was weary;   his wasted blade
    failed,
Futile for fighting,   and that for the first time—
It was a great and good blade.   Grim and not easy
Was the path of Ecgtheow's heir,   answering fate
As he left home and hall,   a home far off to seek,   2590

144

Gone from the good earth   to gain his everlasting hall,
As all men must,   leaving middle earth behind,
And their leasehold on life—   Not long after
Those combatants closed again,   and clashed in fury.
That hoard-guard took heart,   exhaling heat and fire,
Swelled up with a second wind,   and the struggle was joined again,
And Beowulf was in the blaze,   that brave ruler of Geats.
His comrades lost courage,   his comrades all bolted,
Born of nobles, they bolted,   all bested by fear.
2600 They wavered in warfare,   to the woods they all fled,
To save their sorry lives.   One single retainer
Felt the sorrows of sympathy—   that sign of true kinship
Will not wester or waver   in a worthy mind.

At this crucial moment, with Beowulf engulfed in flames, his men desert him and run—all but one.

Reading 11
Questions

Make sure you double-check your answers in the back of the book.

1. What are some ways in which Beowulf seems to be cast as a Christ figure in this section?

2. Do you notice anything Tolkien is borrowing from Anglo-Saxon culture? Make a note of anything you see.

Thirty-sixth Fitt
Wiglaf's speech, rally, Beowulf wounded

Weohstan's son, Wiglaf, was that wise thane remaining,
A solid shield-bearer, a Scylfing prince,
Kinsman or cousin to Aelfhere. His king he saw struggling,
His helmet heated terribly, the fight going hard for him.
He brought to mind memories, the marvels his lord had gifted him,
Wealthy holdings, wide halls for the Waegmunding tribe,

Notice what Wiglaf remembers here at this critical moment.

2610 Keeps and common lands that were kept by his father.
It was too hard to hold back. He held up his yellow linden shield,
He seized his great sword, from the scabbard he drew it—
Eanmund, son of Ohtere, had that heirloom at first,
And he was slain in some slaughter, struck down by Weohstan,
Friendless in futile exile, he fought and he lost.
So Weohstan won for his kin the war gear of Eanmund,
A bright, burnished helmet, a breastplate of woven rings,
A grip hilt for giants, all given to Onela,
Who, tested, returned them, which told of his mercy;
2620 He knew that his nephew was the noble who fell,

But he refused the feud,   and favored Weohstan.
For many winters Weohstan kept it,   this war-gear he won,
Chain mail and choice shield,   till his chosen son was grown,
And wrought feats like his father,   and could fight his own battles.
So he gave him that gear—   with the Geats they lived then—
A huge collection he had conquered,   when he counted out his days,
As old men always do.   Now that eager young warrior,
With his lord and leader,   was a lieutenant strong,
And was called to combat,   the collision of true battle.
His war-wisdom did not waver,   nor was the wish of his lord   2630
Denied in that defense,   as the drake soon found out
When those foes finally fought   and finished the matter.
Wiglaf spoke wisely,   and his words were fitting,
As he, grieved and grim,   said gravely to his comrades,
"My mind full remembers,   when mead was given to us,
And the proud hall-promises   that our prince heard from us.
He gave us rings; we were resolute,   we refused to dishonor him.
We promised our pride,   we professed our deep loyalty.
For helmets and hard edges,   we held out allegiance
For strife of this sort.   And so he selected us   2640
From his entire army   to enlist with him here.
He called us companions,   covered us with gifts,

The bond between ring-giver and thanes goes back to the mead-hall. He gave rings, they swore loyalty. Now is the moment where they have to show their faithfulness.

Wiglaf reminds them they were handpicked by Beowulf as the most courageous and loyal thanes.

Considering and counting us   to have courage with the spear,
To be good in grim battle,   and grave in our helmets.
Our courageous king   had counted on being alone,
Our fighting folk-king   wanted to finish alone,
He has gathered glory,   great among men
For deeds of great daring.   But the day is upon us
When our lord and leader   needs lieutenants, stout-hearted.

2650   Bring our strength, let us stand with him!   Let us strike at the dragon;
Let us help our hero-king   while the heat is upon him,
Fiery and fierce.   For God is witness
I would fare far better   if the fire took me
Together with our good king,   a gift of honorable death.
It would hardly be right, horrible,   if hanging our heads,
We carried craven shields home,   cowards all of us,
Instead of standing firm   and struggling to save
The life of our Weder lord.   The laws of honor
Forbid our bold king   to brave it alone,

2660   To be the good Geat warrior   who gave us his strength,
And sank in the strife.   This sword and this helmet,
Breastplate, bold shield   will be better for both of us."
Through the furious fumes   he fought his way forward,
Bringing his battle-helmet,   and briefly said,
"Beowulf, dear and dauntless,   do what you do,
As when young, yearning for glory,   you vowed great things,
Saying you would not waver,   and that while life was in you,

Your glory would not go.   Now, great in heroics,
Prince of high prowess,   protect your life
With all your stated strength.   I will stand here with you."   2670
At those daring, dauntless words,   the dragon came again,
Eager and angry,   and with envious rage,
Uncoiling in cruelty,   its courageous hated ones to seek,
The fire unfurled,   the flames came in waves,
And burned down to the boss,   the breastplate also failed
To protect the young prince,   who empowered with courage,
Went quickly under his kinsman's shield,   keeping faith,
Since his own emblem   was eaten by fire,
All burned to blazes.   The brave king again
Called to mind and memory   the might of his glory,   2680
Thrust his striking sword   at the serpent's head,
A blow of blunt hatred.   But the blade, Naegling, shattered,
Beowulf's sword broke,   in battle it staggered,
Old and gray ancient.   The edge of the sword
Was fated to fail him;   faltering at great moments
Of struggle and strife.   So strong was his hand,
As the tale was told me,   he tested them hard,
And with the strength of each stroke   he struck them to pieces—
All the blades he would break,   and was no better off.
Then the dread fire dragon   determined to end it   2690
And rushed in his rage   to wreck final vengeance.

Beowulf's own strength works against him. He breaks his weapons and then is left to fight weaponless—which means that he is no better off.

He found an opening finally   and furiously bit
With his fangs in a fury,   and fastened them deep
In the neck of that noble,   in the neck of the hero—
In waves his blood welled,   and he weltered in
   crimson.

Thirty-Seventh Fitt
Wiglaf and Beowulf kill the dragon

I have heard the high courage,   how the great hero,
   Wiglaf,
Helped his king with his courage,   and kept his high
   honor,
With deeds of great daring   and deep honor of nature.
He did not hit at the head,   his hand badly burned,
2700 High-hearted, heroic,   he helped his great king.
He lunged and struck lower   and the loathsome drake
Was struck with that steel;   his sword pierced the
   neck,
A bright, bitter blade,   the blaze of the dragon
Diminished and dimmed.   A desperate stroke
Came from the king,   as he cut with his knife,
A blade from his belt,   by his breastplate kept,
That great Weder warrior   wounded his belly,
Cut him, killed him,   and conquered the dragon.
Kinsmen together killed it,   conquerors both of them.
2710 That's what a thane should be!—   His first thought for
   valor
In day of great danger.   That daring
   accomplishment
Was the king's last conquest,   his last captured glory,
His final work in the world.   The wound festered

immediately,
What that earth-drake inflicted   in his eager malice.
The wound seethed and swelled;   soon Beowulf knew
That his breast was burning,   blood-venomous poison,
The pain of deep poison.   The prince staggered across,
Still wise in his wisdom,   to the wall straight across.
He sat and stared   at the stonework of giants,
Those proud arches and pillars   piled high in wisdom,   2720
Upholding the hall   that held the great dragon.
Then the hand of the hero,   the high-hearted Wiglaf,
Brought blessed water   his brave lord to cool,
Clotted and covered   with conquering blood.
His struggle ceasing,   he unstrapped his helmet.
Bold Beowulf spoke   brief words through his hurt,
His fatal wound that felled him.   He full well knew
His joy was justly departing;   he was joining his fathers,
He had finished his long file   of fleeting days,
His day of doom upon him,   his death was approaching.   2730
"I would give gifts   to a good son of mine—
All these garments, this gear,   I would gladly bestow
If I had a high prince   who could inherit my name.
As a prince of this people   I provided just rule,
Fifty winters of favor.   No fierce invader,
None, not one,   from nations nearby
Would wage war on me,   working their mischief,
Or proud provocations.   At peace, I stayed home
And welcomed the waiting respite,   and I worked no intrigues;
I fought no senseless feuds   and was false in no oaths.   2740
Though a man mortally wounded,   I marvel at

goodness—
No blood guilt besmirches me,   and blessed I am.
Mankind's Ruler restores me,   no wrath rests upon
   me—
As my life is leaving me,   and losses prevail—
For the killing of kin.   Quickly, now go
To take in that treasure   tucked under gray stone,
Bold, beloved Wiglaf,   now that beast lies sleeping,
Cold in his cruelty,   cut off from his treasure.
Go, gather in haste.   I would get a good look
2750 At the golden glory,   the gorgeous treasures,
Take in joy through the gems,   rejoice in my dying,
Made better, not bitter,   as I bestow an inheritance
Of my life and legacy   and the length of my rule."

As he's dying, Beowulf wants to see the rings that he's giving to his people. He is a ring-giver to the end.

Thirty-Eighth Fitt
Beowulf sees the treasure, orders his burial

I don't wonder at this word,   that Weohstan's son
Took the words and wishes   of his wounded king,
And went, although weary,   in his woven chain mail,
Bent into the barrow,   and bravely went in.
Passing the supreme seat,   he saw a vast treasure,
That young kinsman of courage,   caught a glimpse of
   great heaps
2760 Of glistering gold   and gems on the floor.
The wall tapestries were a wonder,   wrought with great
   cunning,
In the den of that drake,   that ancient dawn-flier,
Unburnished beakers   that brave men once held,
Bereft of their richness;   rusty helmets scattered.
Scores of torques in the treasure   told of their

craftsmanship.
Such wealth can rob wisdom,   steal wit from mankind,
Might overcome anyone,   all men are vulnerable.
However you hide it—   heed this fair warning!
Then he glimpsed a gold standard,   great splendor giving,
Above the hoard hanging,   handcraft of wise women,   *2770*
Embroidered and bright,   a brilliant light came from it,
So he took in the treasure floor,   and tasted the wealth,
Viewing their victory.   That cruel victim was dead,
No sign of the serpent;   their swords had dispatched him.
So, that hill I have heard   had its hoard pillaged,
Great gifts from the earth,   what giants had wrought.
One man made his way out,   with many a wonder,
With gold cups, with gold dishes,   and the gold standard,
Bright in its brilliance.   His brave lord's sword,
Edged with hard iron,   had entered the vitals   *2780*
Of the great and grim sentry   of the golden pile,
Who time out of mind, terrible,   that tyrant of greed,
Blew hot and horror,   and held safe his treasure,
Until he died, desolate,   in the dead of the night.
Then this high-hearted hero,   that hoard left behind,
Retracing his true path,   tried in his soul
As to whether the Weder king,   wounded and bleeding,
Would still be lingering alive,   where he had left him above,
Weakening, wounded,   by the wall of gray rock.
So he took out the treasure   and took in the king,   *2790*

Still bleeding, still brave, that bold and great chieftain,
Still losing his lifeblood. Again the lieutenant
Wet his forehead with water— a word finally came out,
Broke from his breast-treasury. Beowulf spoke,
Ancient, elder king, as he eyed all the gold.
"For the gleaming gold here, the great God I thank,
To that worker of wonders, my words are lifted
To Heaven's high Lord, behold, all the treasure!
By the grace of God I give this treasure,
2800 On the day of my death, for a deserving, good people.   *Beowulf passes the kingdom to Wiglaf and the treasure to his people.*
My final breath is bartered, a bargain I call it,
To gain all this gold. Give yourself to the task,
Care for the commonwealth. I can tarry no longer.
Build me a barrow, with all my battle friends,
When the pyre's heat is past on the proud headland,
At the wide Whale Cliff, a witness to glory,
A memorial for men, my memory to keep,
So crews under sail coming by may call it by name,
Calling it Beowulf's barrow, as breezing homeward,
2810 They work their white-throated ships over the wine dark sea."
Then the good king unclasped his great collar of gold,
Gave it with thanks to his thane, with thought to be generous,
Gave his helmet and hard breastplate, and he held out his ring,
And bade him receive with boldness, and with a blessing to use them.
"You are the last living man who is left of our race,
The way of the Waegmundings. Wyrd has taken us all,

All my clan has been conquered   and, kept in their doom,
Great earls in their glory.   I must go to them now."
This word from that warrior   was wisdom at last,
What he wished to say   before the waves of heat   *2820*
From his calling pyre consumed him.   From that courageous heart
His soul was sent out,   a saint's reward to find.

Thirty-Ninth Fitt
Wiglaf Rebukes the Cowardly Thanes

It was a hard hit—   the young hero was staggered
To look down on his lord,   laid out on the earth
With the great, grievous wound   that got him his end.
But the dragon was dead   and done with predation,
That earth-dragon, evil night-flier,   eager in cruelty,
Brave blows struck him dead,   bold were his killers.
That coiled cruelty was done,   and could not keep his treasure.
Iron with hard edges   had ended his life,   *2830*
Brilliant and battle-sharp,   the blunt hammers' labor,
Had felled that high flier,   his flames were all quenched,
Silenced in that slaughter,   its death summons final.
No longer aloft at midnight,   circling left and then right,
Boasting in his blazes,   making brave men quake,
Proud of its prowess,   prideful in wealth,
Felled the hand of the high-hearted king,   that hero and king.
There are hardly any heroes   who could hold their

      own,
      Though stout and steadfast,   as the scops all sing,
2840 With such a poisonous serpent,   against such odds—
      The poisonous breath of that pestilence,   the power of that worm,
      Who might dare that deep cave,   and delve into the rings
      When that watchful worm   was still awake and alive.
      Beowulf was bold   and at the barrow he died.
      The price of life was precious,   precious treasure indeed,
      And both man and monster   met their end at last,
      The end of all days.   After a while
      The cowards crept back   to the cave and to Wiglaf,
      Oath breakers, all of them,   ashamed in their cowardice,
2850 Ten who were tried   and tempted to fear,
      At their lord's final limit,   they left with their spears.
      In shame, their shields lowered,   they shuffled back
      In their metal mail-shirts,   where their manly leader rested,
      And looked at war-weary Wiglaf.   Watching his king,
      He sat by the shoulder,   a stout-hearted thane,
      Still washing him with water,   whether it did good or not.
      However deeply devoted he was,   this death took his king away,
      And he could not keep life   in his courageous king's body,
      Or ward off the will   of the only wise God.
2860 The word that works all things   is the word of the Lord
      For all men, and every man,   as He always does.

Hard words with hard edges   were hot and came easily,
From that courageous young courtier   to cowards standing there.
Wiglaf spoke wisely,   Weohstan's son,
A grieved and good man,   to those who had gone running,
"To tell all the truth,   this tale is easy enough—
This ring-giving ruler   who richly rewarded you
With battle gear, bucklers,   and hilts embossed well,
Whose mind would remember   his mead-bench retainers
And in his hall would give helmets   and well-hardened breastplates,   *2870*
As lord to lieutenants,   the loveliest weapons
Whether far off he found them,   or found them at home,
They were wasted on these warriors,   weapons just thrown away,
Given to men who gave no battle,   who would rather grovel than fight.
Our bold king could not boast   of brave comrades in arms,
But the Ruler of victory, the Righteous one,   gave revenge to his arm.
God gave him great strength   and grace for battle,
So that with solitary sword   in the strife he prevailed.
To assist in that struggle,   to save his life,
There was little or less   my lord could expect from me,   *2880*
But I managed to maim the drake,   but little more to help my king.
Its energy ebbed,   the eager fire dimmed

> When I struck with my sword   that beast was slower than he was.
> When manly courage should remain,   you men were off in the woods,
> In throes of thick battle,   you thought to run off.
> Now the giving of gifts   and the goods of exchanging,
> The joys of hall and hearth,   and all home-delights,
> Shall fade from families,   your freeholds taken,
> Your clansman and kinfolk   will be caught up in exile,
2890 > When distant nobles deny   that such a deed should be ignored,
> Hearing of your feckless flight,   inflamed with indignation.
> No, death is a good deal better   than deserting your king,
> Which for a lord's lieutenant   is a life of shame."

The cowards will be expelled from the mead-hall, and there are no ring-givers anywhere who will take them on.

Reading 12
Questions

Make sure you double-check your answers in the back of the book.

1. What is the poet doing here with the themes of valor and treasure? What is the relationship between the two? What is the point of each?

2. The blood-avenger has been a theme throughout the poem. What is the interesting twist on this in the death of Beowulf?

3. What is the fate of the rest of the company?

4. Do you notice anything Tolkien is borrowing from Anglo-Saxon culture? Make a note of anything you see.

Fortieth Fitt
Wiglaf expects trouble and broods

    Then he calmly commanded   that the conquest be announced
    To those retainers on the ridge   who had rested in sorrow
    All that morning, meditating;   men of nobility,
    Holding shields, shaking their heads,   summoning doubts.
    Would they welcome their lord home   or bewail his loss?
    The herald sent held nothing back,   though it hurt to announce.
2900   The tidings were told,   and the tale was full,
    By the herald who rode up the headland   and held forth.
    "Now the wise ruler of Weders,   who willingly gave gifts,
    On his deathbed lies dedicated,   that great defender of Geats,
    He sleeps fast, slaughtered   by the serpent's malice.
    Beside him, that man-slaying monster   remembers nothing,
    Done in by dagger strokes,   this was not done with swords,
    No blow from a long blade   sliced the beast open."
    So Wiglaf, Weohstan's son,   sat wondering
    By the brave-hearted Beowulf,   beside his dead lord,

Wiglaf warns them of the coming war. As soon as the news of Beowulf's death spreads, all their old enemies will re-surface. Remember how Hygelac attacked the Frisians? They will surely seize this opportunity, as well as the Swedes, who also have an old grudge.

A still-living leader beside a lord who died valiantly, 2910
And a heart-heavy watch by two heads keeps vigil,
Over dead friend and dead foe, both dead together.
"Our people must prepare themselves, prepare for battle—
When the Frisians and Franks hear of the fall of our king,
When that message makes its way across many lands.
Remember how Hygelac harried his enemies,
Taking his fleet to the Frisians, and fled from them there.
The Hetware humbled him, hitting him hard in battle,
Avenging the wrong with vaster force, victory was easily theirs,
And our bold battle-leader was bent beneath them, 2920
Falling in the fighting. No more favor in ring-giving
From that faithful leader and lord. And from that time
The Merovingian men brought their malice against us.
Nor do I expect eagerness for accepting peace
From the Swedes and some others. It was said far and wide
That the anger of Ongentheow attacked his enemy's life,
Haethcyn, son of Hrethel, who lost hope and life at Ravenswood,
When Geats in great pride sought glory in battle against
The best of the Battle-Scylfings. Soon the boldness of Ohtere,
Aged but eager, old but cunning, 2930

Struck back with a blow,   and beat the sea-king,
Killing him coldly,   and his queen taking back.
He rescued that rich wife,   though bereft of her wealth,
Mother of Ohtere and Onela,   aged queen.
Then he hunted his hostile foes,   his hated enemy,
Sore pressed and pressured,   he pursued them hotly,
They barely made it back,   beating their retreat to Ravenswood.
With his high-hearted host,   he held siege for the survivors.
The wound-weary men,   wretched, had made it to refuge.

2940 But all night he angered them   by attacking with words, saying,
In the morning some men   would be mown down by swords,
And some would swing   on the sullen gallows-tree,
As ravens' delight, ravenous birds.   But rescue was timely
When the day dawned   for those despairing men
And they heard the great horn   of Hygelac's company,
The free timbre of his trumpet;   with troops behind him,
Their loyal leader   led men to the rescue.

Forty-First Fitt
Hygelac kills Ongentheow, the Swedes will be back.

"There was a swath of Swedes,   a bloody swath of Geats,
A trail of blood and trial,   talked about everywhere;

Wiglaf is reminiscing, reminding us of the bad blood that exists between the Geats and the Swedes. There are two blood-feuds that have been on pause for a while. The Geats vs. Swedes, and the Geats vs. Frisians. Remember how Beowulf had said before his death that he had participated in no senseless feuds. (Line 2739) He had been the peacekeeper, but now he's gone. All of the old grudges will come back to the surface.

How those two tribes   tore into each other.   2950
Then the aged Ongentheow,   eager for respite,
Sought out a stronghold,   foreseeing great trouble.
So he sought out a citadel,   seeking his refuge.
He knew Hygelac was hale,   and a hard man in battle,
He knew his pride and his prowess,   a powerful fighter,
So he sought out safety   from those sea-wandering fighters.
The king had no confidence   he could keep his great treasure,
His kingly sons and his queen,   so he quit him again,
Aged one, to his earthwall.   Hot after him came
The high banners of Hygelac   that were held over the field,   2960
With the battle plain bloodied,   and the Geats had the better of it
Till the brave and bold Hrethelings   breached the walls of the town.
Ongentheow, battling boldly,   was brought to bay,
Grim and gray-headed,   he gripped his sword fiercely,
And fought Eofer's fury,   that fighting king was backed against it.
Against his enemy's anger,   who attacked the king.
Wulf, Wonred's son,   swung his weapon hard,
And blood spurted in streams,   surging from beneath his hair.
But the sturdy old Scyfing   stood firmly without fear,
And a blow came straight back   with a blade of vengeance.   2970
Wulf got the worst of it   as their weapons flew,
And he faced his foe   with fierce intentions.
Wonred's son was not swift enough   as he summoned

    his answer
To deliver with daring   to that doughty king.
He took a hit to the head;   his helmet was split—
He bent toward earth, bloodied,   as bravely he fell.
The blow was deadly, he fell down,   but his doom was not yet,
That edge entered him deep,   but he after recovered.
Then Eofer the fierce,   a fighting thane for Hygelac,
2980 When his bold brother fell,   swung his blade in anger,
An old, ancient giant blade   that entered great helmets.
Over the shield wall, he shattered the helmet   and shuttered that king,
The old shepherd fell, fatally struck,   forever fallen,
He left his aged life,   at the last fell to the ground.
The brother's wounds were bound;   they brought him up,
Raised him upright,   righting him when there was space
For them to keep and control   what they had conquered in war.
Eofor took off Ongentheow   the iron breastplate,
Warrior from warrior,   taking weapons also,
2990 Hilted sword and helmet,   a hard edge captured.
He took them heroically to Hygelac,   holding the grayhead's armor,
Who received them royally   and registered his promises
To reward them handsomely at home,   and held his word firmly.
For great deeds in grim battle,   the Geat lord was generous,

High-hearted, son of Hrethel,   when home was theirs,
To warriors Eofor and Wulf   gave a wealth of great
   riches,
One hundred thousand high honors,   in hearth-land
   and rings.
No man resented the riches,   it was reckoned well
   worth it,
As these men were mighty,   marvelous in battle.
And Eofor he honored,   eagerly gave his one daughter,   *3000*
The grace of his great house,   the gift of his home.
This is the feud I fear,   the ferocity of tribes,
When the Swedes are summoned   by our sorrowful
   loss,
And come in their cruelty,   seeking conquest and
   pillage,
For this fatal fight of theirs,   the fell-Scylfings,
When they learn of our loss,   that our lord lies dead,
Who led us in life,   and gave lands and treasures,
And defended them fighting   from our foes and
   enemies.
He fell, his life's clasp fastened,   he finished his race
A hero high-hearted.   Let us hasten now,   *3010*
As we gaze on our Geat lord,   as we go to mourn him,
And carry the king,   who collected rings for giving,
To the bier we have built   for Beowulf our lord.
No small bits shall burn   with his bones together.
Great gems and gold,   glittering jewels without
   number,
A treasure torn free   by that trial taking his life.
The blaze will take the booty,   let the burning fire eat
   it.
No warrior can willingly carry   the work-craft found

They're going to burn the treasure on Beowulf's pyre. Remember all the treasure heaped on Shield at his death? They pushed a dead king loaded with treasure out to sea; here they commit a dead king heaped with treasure to the flames.

here.
No lady of loveliness   will light up her radiance
3020 With a tempting torque for the neck,   twisted in gold.
No, she will never walk at home,   but benighted in exile,
With her gladness gone,   gold stolen, she will walk alone,
Just as our lifeless leader   has lost all his joys,
All lightness and laughter.   Many a lifted spear
Shall greet the grim cold mornings,   shall be gripped for battle,
And hefted in scarred hands;   no harp will play
To wake the warriors.   But the wan-dark raven
Feasts on the fallen,   with puffed feathers he boasts
To the enticed eagle   how he ate without measure,
3030 As raven and ravening wolf   were rending the bodies."
So the herald held forth   with hurting words;
He did not deceive,   his deed was true.
Weary in heart, the warriors rose   and wound their way,
Mourning, they made their way,   up the mound to Eagle Cliff.
The men all went, weeping,   the wonder to see.
They found him still, on the sand,   stretched out in death,
Their leader, now lifeless,   he who had lavished gold
On heroes in happier days.   His halting day had come,
It had dawned on this daring one;   death had come to the king,
3040 A good and great king,   and a glorious death.
Beside the king was the conquered worm,   his cruelty ceased,

Lying next to their lord,   still loathsome in death,
His scales scorched,   this serpent of fire,
Laid out like lumber,   his light and fire gone.
It was fifty feet long,   the full measure of hate,
Laid out grim on the ground.   Its glory was
   night-flying,
Seeking its den only at dawn,   but death had him now,
Held firm forever   in the fist of cold death.
He lost his lease   on that low earth hall.
Scattered and strewn about   were stacks of bowls,   3050
   cups,
Dishes with inlaid decorations,   and jewel bedecked
   swords,
Wrecked and rust-bitten,   resting on the lap of the
   earth,
Waiting a thousand winters,   wasting away.
For that large legacy,   that left behind gold,
By ancient, honorable men,   was edged with a spell,
Leaving the treasure untouchable,   temptation out of
   reach,
For any humble human soul,   unless Heaven's-Ruler,
The great God Himself,   might give it away
As Protector of princes,   the priceless hoard to bestow
To such a man as seemed   most suitable to him.   3060

This ancient giant treasure had been protected by a spell. No one could touch it unless God himself gave it to a worthy man.

FORTY-SECOND FITT
CURSED TREASURE EXAMINED

It proved perilous indeed   for the poor soul who came
To hide in that hall,   hiding from justice.
Its guardian was grim   and got his revenge.
In cruelty he killed one of us,   and the king retaliated,

But that deed was dire.   Dread wonder strikes—
How might a man   of magnificent strength
Come to life's limit,   when that lord no longer
May laugh in the mead-hall   with merry friends.
So Beowulf, that brave one,   when the barrow-guard he fought
3070 A conflict deeply contested,   he could not know
In what manner of men   he should leave middle-earth at last.
Princes their curses pronounced,   those who put the gold there,
And damned until doomsday   the desperate fool
So that man might be marked   with measurements for sin,
Held with hell-chains   and horrors plenty,
Torments testing him,   who should take from that hoard.
That gracious king was not greedy,   but the grace of heaven
Was what the king in his kindness   had kept in mind.
Wiglaf, son of Weohstan,   spoke words from the heart,
3080 "One destiny for warriors,   as wisdom shows us
Is suffering and sorrow,   and so we submit to it.
Our courageous king   our counsel rejected,
Our beloved lord   left our petitions aside.
That guardian of greed   should have gone unmolested,
Should have been left alone, lying   in that lair of sin,
Kept in that cold cavern   till the climax of the world,
But he held to his high course,   and the hoard is now ours,
Though we paid a precious price;   that penalty is grievous

Beowulf wasn't greedy—the treasure wasn't what he was there for. He was there for his people, and because of this he gained the treasure. In a way, this is similar to him discovering the secret to killing Grendel. He renounced weapons for other reasons, but that turned out to be the only possible way he could defeat the monster. In this case, the only way to gain the treasure was to not be there for the treasure.

For the task which took   our tale-rich king and lord.
I went down to that weird chamber   where I saw the   *3090*
  gold,
Mounds of magnificent treasure,   when the moment
  was given me,
A gift not easily granted, to go down there,
Under the earth-fortress.   With bold eagerness, I
  seized
As much from those mounds   as a man can carry,
And hurried back in haste   to my high prince.
My lord and leader . . .   alive he still was,
Waiting in wise patience,   his wit still active.
In sorrow he spoke   and said to greet you.
He said to build him a bier   when his breath was gone,
Where we burn his bones,   the barrow should be high,   *3100*
A magnificent memorial,   massive and worthy of him.
He was the best of the brave ones,   the boldest of men,
During his days,   when he dealt out rings.
Let us go down the great hole   a grim second time
And search out these stores   of silver and gold,
Wondrous delights, strange devices,   down we will go,
Where you may gaze at the gold,   glimpsing splendor,
Bracelets and brave jewels.   Let the bier be fashioned
  now,
Ready to roar   when we return to the surface.
We must carry our king,   our courageous prince—   *3110*
Beloved lord!   Where the long days begin,
Safe from all sorrow,   in the shelter God's keeping."
Then Wiglaf, son of Weohstan,   gave words of
  command
To his fierce fighters,   to his faithful men
Who owned their own lands,   to urgently bring

Wood to feed the fire;   the flames would be hungry
At the funeral of that famous king.   "Now fire shall eat,
And dark flames devour   our devoted leader,
Who would stand steadfast   when struggle was joined,
3120   Under the arch of arrows,   when anger loosed them,
And they came cunningly;   keeping the shaft
And the flocked feathers,   and the fatal head all together."
The son of Weohstan, full of sense,   said he would choose
Seven wise warriors,   wizened and great-hearted,
The bravest and best   formed the band to descend.
He, the eighth warrior, eagerly led;   the entrance swallowed them.
He held a lit torch aloft   and led the way down
Under the evil roof   of that iniquitous hall.
No lots were allowed   for the looting privilege;
3130   They saw in a moment how much there was,   how many piles,
With no serpent for a sentry,   and all scattered about.
They lost little time,   leaving nothing behind,
And they hauled it out with heavy loads   and heavy hearts.
The deadly treasure cost them dear.   The dragon they dragged
To the cold cliff-edge,   committing it to water,
The surf swallowed him,   a now silent carcass.
Then torques and entwined gold pieces   were tossed into wagons,
Riches beyond reckoning.   The royal one was carried,
Kingly, in quiet majesty,   to the Cape of Whales.

Forty-Third Fitt
Funeral of Beowulf, no hope

Then the Geats in their grief,   having gathered the wood,   *3140*
Assembled an impressive pyre   and piled treasure on it.
Helmets were hanging there,   harnesses and shields,
Breastplates burnished,   as he had bidden them.
In the midst they laid their marvelous king,   mighty prince,
Great heroes grieving   their good master gone.
Then for the king they kindled   a colossal blaze,
Clouds of smoke curled upward,   closing the sky,
Black smoke, blaze red,   and blending in sorrow
Was the crackling fire and keening people—   quiet was the wind—
Until the body burst   and the bones were blackened   *3150*
By the great heat at the heart of it.   With hurting spirits,
They grieved in great sorrow   at their good lord's passing.
An old Weder widow   wailed in grief,

Her hair coiled for the king,   a keening prophetess,
She sang sorrowfully   and said what she feared.
She dreaded doom of battle,   the days to come
Would be devastating, deadly,   dark and shameful.
There would be sorrow and sadness.   The sky drank the smoke.
The Weder Geats worked   and when done,
There was a barrow on the bluff,   broad and high,   *3160*
Easily seen by seafarers,   those sent from afar.

It took them ten days,   and the tomb was prepared
For the brave battle-king.   They built walls for his
  ashes,
The ramparts of royalty,   a righteous tribute,
The best they could build   with their better artisans.
They brought to the barrow   the booty, that treasure,
All the baubles and bracelets   that had been brought
  before
From that hoard by heroes,   by hostiles or friends.
They gave to the ground   a great treasure indeed,
3170 Gold in the ground,   a gift to the silence,
As useless now as it used to be,   as useless now as it
  ever was.
Then around that barrow brave men rode,
  battle-tested,
Champions, chieftains,   twelve children of
  princes,
To lament their lost king,   to lift their respect,
To keen their cold dirge,   to collect their honor.
They praised his princely rule,   his power and kindness;
They deemed him devoted.   They did well.
Men should praise masters   when masters do well,
And hold up high praise   when they have to depart
3180 From this life of loss   to the life everlasting.
Thus the Geats grieved   and gave a great mourning
For the loss of their leader,   kind lord and ring-giver.
A captain of kings,   they called him beloved,
Of men the mildest,   and most respected,
Kind to his clansmen,   and keen for true honor.

Notice that the poem ends the way it began—with the funeral of a great king. A woman is wailing at the pyre, like the woman who wailed at the pyre at Finnsburg. Their hero is gone; their enemies surround them.

Reading 13
Questions

Make sure you double-check your answers in the back of the book.

1. The entire poem ends with the death of our hero, and a recounting of all the long-standing feuds which will now return with a vengeance. They are all sorrowing, and their enemies are all around them. Why do you think the poet is leaving us at this point in the story?

2. Do you notice anything Tolkien is borrowing from Anglo-Saxon culture?

Now that you've completed both books, it's time to review before you take your test. You'll need to study the information from your poetry workbook, make sure that you have the memorization done, and understand all the study questions at the end of each day's reading. It is also, of course, assumed that you have a basic understanding of the plot, characters, themes, etc. The test questions will be mostly matching, short answer, fill-in-the-blank, and one essay.

There are two more essays included next, but the information from these will not be on the test. If you find yourself interested in Beowulf *or in Anglo-Saxon it is highly recommended that you read them. They are both by Douglas Wilson, whose versification of* Beowulf *you have just finished reading. The first essay is about the Christianity of the poem, the second is about the structure of the poem, and both essays will make you quite a bit smarter.*

Beowulf: The UnChrist
Douglas Wilson

The poetry of *Beowulf* is not just an artistic triumph, although it certainly is that. As the themes of *Beowulf* are carefully considered and weighed, it should also be considered as an evangelistic and apologetic *tour de force*.[1]

Both the pagan and Christian elements in the poem are obvious and readily visible, and much scholarly debate has raged over the relationship between them and what to do about the tension that these two elements create for one another in the poem. Usually the sides choose up according to whether they believe the paganism is fundamental to the worldview of the poem, with Christian elements sprinkled on top, or whether the Christian elements are fundamental, with the paganism (inexplicably) sprinkled on top. In both cases, the tension is frequently treated as an accidental by-product of poetic incompetence or inadequate redaction of two or more different sources.

I want to argue here that the two elements were placed in tension by the poet deliberately, and that he did this in order to accomplish a stunning apologetic for the Christian faith. The result is a powerful *praeparatio ad conversionem*. The *Beowulf* poet is not syncretistic in his inclinations at all. He is not like one of those backsliding monks at Lindisfarne, sternly rebuked by Alcuin for paying attention to the ancient heroic tales:

"What has Ingeld to do with Christ? The house is narrow, it cannot contain both. The king of the heavens will have nothing to do with heathen and damned so-called kings. For the eternal king rules in the heavens, the lost heathen repines in hell."[2]

But our poet is not a conflicted monk at that particular *minster*, reading James Joyce under the covers at night with a flashlight. The paganism that is so evident throughout this poem is presented to us by a thoroughly

---
1. This essay appeared in a shorter form some years ago in *Touchstone* magazine. That shorter form can be accessed here: http://www.touchstonemag.com/archives/article.php?id=20-06-030-f.
2. As quoted in Paul Cavill, *Anglo-Saxon Christianity* (London: HarperCollins, 1999), 57. It is most interesting (at least to me) that Alcuin mentions Ingeld here, a minor character in *Beowulf*.

Christian poet, and he does not show us this paganism in order to say, "See, pagans can be noble, too—even without Jesus!" Rather, he is doing precisely the opposite—he is refusing to engage in a fight with a heathen straw man of his own devising. He acknowledges the high nobility that was there, but then he bluntly shows us that nobility *at the point of profound despair.* The effect is extremely potent. Instead of saying that nobility is possible without Christ, the poet is showing that without Christ, such nobility does not keep a people from being utterly and completely *lost.* To adapt a comment made by C. S. Lewis about Homer, the gray granite of pagan nobility in the poem is polished to shine like marble, but it is still granite for all that. This is nobility at the end of its tether.

In this approach the poet is taking his cue from the apostle Paul. When St. Paul attacks the "natural man" (1 Corinthians 2:14) he is *not* taking on all the drug addicts, winos, and hookers of Corinth. Rather, he is referring to man at his best—yachtsman, advisor to kings and presidents, philosopher, harpsichord player, and war hero. *That* was the man who did not "know God" (1 Corinthians 1:21). St. Paul was taking on the Corinthian aristocracy, and something very similar is happening here.

The *Beowulf* poet is not seeking to praise paganism in order to make any room for it. His task is far more profound. Paganism at its best, at its *most* noble and heroic, was still without hope and without God in the world. If paganism at its best and most aristocratic was a really fine car, the *Beowulf* poet climbs into it and drives it into a tree.

The action of the poem is on both sides of AD 521, taking this hard date from Gregory of Tours's mention of Hygelac's disastrous raid on the Frisians. The conversion of the Anglo-Saxons to the Christian faith began in earnest about seventy years later, in the 590s. "During three or four generations starting in the 590s, all the English kings and their courts converted to Christianity."[3] Not only so, but we also know from history that both the Danes and the Geats (if they existed) were unconverted pagans at

---

3. John Blair, *The Anglo-Saxon Age* (Oxford: Oxford University Press, 1984), 23.

the time of Hygelac.⁴

If we place the *Beowulf* poet in the early eighth century, this is just one century after the Anglo-Saxons began this process and only about fifty years after it was generally concluded. "By 660 only the men of Sussex and the Isle of Wight remained pagan, and soon they too were converted."⁵ This is just one generation. To place it in an analogous context, my father-in-law was wounded in the battle of Guadalcanal in the Second World War. I am a fifty-year-old man,⁶ easily able to visit with him about the details of that battle, a battle that was sixty-one years before. In short, the *Beowulf* poet could easily have known individual Christian Anglo-Saxons who had converted from paganism. In fact, the poet's own parents could easily have been in that position. That world was dead and gone, but it was not necessarily "long ago and far away."

So their conversion from paganism was not "old news" for them. Paganism was still the faith of numerous other European tribes and peoples, and the time of Anglo-Saxon paganism was still within living memory. Further, the dates of Hygelac's raid and the beginning of the conversion process place the central events of *Beowulf* as the swan song of paganism. It is too easy for us to see that the Christian faith has not yet arrived in the world of *Beowulf*. Nevertheless, the first audience knew that it was just *about* to arrive, and that the world described in that poem was a world that was shortly to pass away. A comparable situation would be created if we were to compose an epic poem about Czar Nicolas. There is no way to hide from a modern audience the fact that the whole thing is about a man whose days and dynasty are numbered. Everyone would know about the great unspoken sequel.

Being on the verge of such a transformation would not be universally true for any given pagan tribe throughout the history of paganism. But in *this* poem, these were pagans on the verge of converting, whether they

---

4. Paul Cavill, *Anglo-Saxon Christianity* (London: HarperCollins, 1999), 116.
5. Blair, 25.
6. Well, I was when I first wrote this. It was true *then*.

were aware of this or not (and they were not). Their historical context at that time was quite different from their own history several centuries before this, and from that of the other tribes that remained pagan for a long time afterwards. The pagan Frisians took Hygelac's life in 521 (when everyone in that region was a heathen), and in AD 755 they were *still* pagan when they murdered St. Boniface. In short, the Frisians were *not* on the threshold of conversion in this poem. But the central tribes in question were.

So some pagans were in transition, but not all of them. The life of freebooting piracy was one that appealed to many ancient pagan tribes. There are numerous accounts of many raiders throughout that ancient European world who entered into their piratical duties with enthusiasm and verve, never giving any of it a second thought. Speaking of the ancient Irish, Thomas Cahill notes, "The characters of the *Tain* do not think profoundly; they do not seem to think at all. But they do act—and with a characteristic panache and roundedness that easily convinces us of their humanity."[7] This is a humanity, all right, but it is not a *reflective* humanity. In short, there are many generations of roistering pillagers who do not appear to think any other lifestyle is either possible or desirable. But in *Beowulf*, this lifestyle of raids and counter-raids, of vengeance accomplished and vengeance thwarted, is a way of life that is very evidently on its last legs. They are (most of them) heartily sick of it, and they keep trying to find ways of fixing the problems caused by the cycles of blood vengeance. Their vain attempts to weave peace, their frustrated attempts to stay the violence with the *wergild*, show that they know they have a serious problem. Their long-established way of doing things gives them all the civilization-building power of a biker gang. It is hard for us to imagine Viking angst, but I want to argue that the author of *Beowulf* is delivering us a vision of exactly that.

---

7. Thomas Cahill, *How the Irish Saved Civilization* (New York: Doubleday, 1995), 76.

One other chronological note is worth mentioning. Hygelac dies circa 520, and Beowulf succeeds his son (who ruled only briefly) and then reigns for fifty years. This brings us down to the 570s, just a few decades before the Anglo-Saxons begin turning to the Christian faith. They are abandoned there by the poet (deliberately, I would argue) on the very threshold of conversion, like a waif left on the doorstep of an orphanage. The aesthetic impact of this is profound. Ovid taught us that it is art to conceal art. And so the poet has done this, but he has concealed it in much the same way that Poe's hero hid the purloined letter, by leaving it out in plain sight. The evangelistic and apologetic impact of this poem is not obvious, but only in the same way that the sky is not obvious.

At the end of the poem, the future is extremely dark, according to Wiglaf, and there is no hope whatever. The Geats now have tons of treasure and no king. Oh, good. Why would an intelligent Christian poet leave them there? The answer is that both he and his audience knew the sequel. And so do we, but perhaps we need to take a closer look at his timing. This poet really knows his business. Speaking of certain elements of the older heroic code and the new faith, Tolkien says this: "And in the poem I think we may observe not confusion, a half-hearted or a muddled business, but a fusion that has occurred at a given point of contact, between old and new, a product of thought and deep emotion."[8]

This fusion is not given to us in order to create a third way between the Christian faith and paganism. We can say this of the *Beowulf* poet— "one thing he knew clearly: those days were heathen—heathen, noble, and hopeless."[9] In this respect, I think that Martin Camargo gets it exactly right: "By linking that past to Old Testament history, by making clear that the hero is the best of men acting in strict accordance with the best rules of conduct then available to him, and finally by showing how far even this exemplary pagan's beliefs fall short of the Christian ideal, the

---

8. J.R.R. Tolkien, *The Monsters and the Critics* (London: HarperCollins, 1997), 20.
9. Tolkien, 22.

poet instead forces his audience to recognize, and thence to abhor the lingering vestiges of paganism in their own hearts."[10]

In order to accomplish this, the poet has to treat certain issues very delicately. But this delicacy is for aesthetic reasons, and not because he is embarrassed by his faith. Rather, he is allowing his pagan characters to be embarrassed by *theirs*. What the *Beowulf* poet is doing is a powerful statement of his faith. But to make this statement, he has to show the characters sympathetically, so that a Christian audience cares what happens to them. At the same time, he has to show that they are in need of Christ and salvation—that which makes them sympathetic does not in any way earn them salvation. There is (probably) salvation for Beowulf himself, but this is an ambiguous hope, not stated clearly. The reasons for this should be become obvious shortly.

The poet gives us an interesting amalgam. The paganism with which we are asked to be in sympathy is more like the worldview of the Jews in the Old Testament than it is like that of the pagans of northern Europe. These noble pagans are monotheistic throughout; they are capable of backsliding into *crude* idolatry; they are well-versed in the ancient parts of the *Old* Testament; they are totally oblivious to the name of Christ; they follow the Old Law (*ealde riht*); they have no priests in their midst, Christian or otherwise; and their culture, their way of life, marriage and war, is identical to that of their ancestors. But there is this one great difference: *they want out*—although they are not yet out.

It is important to emphasize that this kind of "paganism" did not really exist anywhere. In some respects, it is like both Beowulf and Melchizedek—without genealogy, father or mother, beginning of days or end of life.[11]

10. Martin Camargo, "The Finn Episode and the Tragedy of Revenge in *Beowulf*," *Studies in Philology* 78, no. 5 (1981), 134.
11. I know, unlike Melchizedek, Beowulf does have a (minimal) genealogy. But it *is* minimal, and it is that way for a reason. Another point is worth remarking on: Beowulf is a dramatic and fictional character, not a mythological one. But even on the supposedly clear distinction between a historical character (like Hrothgar) and a mythological one (like his great-grandfather Shield), I must confess myself a dubious agnostic. I keep in mind Ambrose Bierce's wonderful definition of mythology, which is the "body of a primitive people's beliefs concerning its origin, early history, heroes, deities and so forth, as distinguished from the true accounts which

Beowulf is an ahistorical character, surrounded by real-life, real-time historical characters. It is the same with the *religion* of Hrothgar and Beowulf—*that* did not exist anywhere either. This is a dramatic device. It enables a Christian audience to be sympathetic (which they would *not* be to paganism *tout court*), and at the same time it provides something to sympathize *with*. This culture is pagan enough to need Christ desperately, and not so pagan as to arouse the contempt of the audience. It is striking that in order to get this paganism "at its best," the *Beowulf* poet had to make it up, just as he had to make up a hero who exemplified all the heroic virtues. All the identifiable historical characters in this poem had significant flaws. The one king who does not is Beowulf, the one who cannot be found in the historical record anywhere else.

In this way, the poet is like Beowulf himself when he disdained to fight Grendel with a sword. The poet could have rejected paganism simply, dispatching it with the sword of the Spirit, in the name of Christ. But he does not use weapons—he grapples with paganism at its best, and tears off its right arm. But I am beginning to allegorize . . .

I said a moment ago that the worldview of this "pagan" society was more like that of the Jews in the Old Testament than it was like that of real, live pillaging pagans. While this is true enough, it has to be noted that this is a comparative statement, and not a claim that Beowulf was at all Mosaic. The *ealde riht* mentioned as that law which Beowulf worries that he has violated (line 2332)[12] does not appear to be anything like the Ten Commandments.[13] Not only is there no specific mention of the New Testament in *Beowulf*, there is also no mention of any Old Testament book besides Genesis. And yet, *Beowulf* is filled with references to the book of Genesis. So this does not appear to be a contrast between natural revelation and special revelation. Rather, the pagans here have a very limited amount of special revelation, but what they *do* have, they refer to

---

it invents later." Ambrose Bierce, *The Devil's Dictionary* (New York: Dover Publications, 1958), 90.

12. Unless otherwise noted, all line numbers are from this edition.

13. It also does not seem to me to be anything like the medieval understanding of "natural law." Natural law is *timeless*, and this law is *ancient*. And Beowulf seems to be as unlike Boethius as a man can be.

frequently. Cain is mentioned (108). The Flood is mentioned (1691). The giants that rebelled against God are mentioned (113).

In such a context, it seems reasonable to me to postulate that the *ealde riht* that Beowulf suddenly worries about after the dragon attack is the ancient Noahic covenant that was made just after the Flood, also from Genesis. After the Flood, God makes a covenant with all mankind (*not* just with the Jews). The rainbow is the sign of that covenant, and the terms of the covenant to be kept by man are found in that book as well. "And surely your blood of your lives will I require; at the hand of every beast will I require it, and at the hand of man; at the hand of every man's brother will I require the life of man. Whoso sheddeth man's blood, by man shall his blood be shed: for in the image of God made he man" (Genesis 9:5–6).

Beowulf, for all his nobility, is still a man of blood. Man is created in the *imago Dei*, and God will require it of us when we shed blood. It should be noted that Beowulf was not a murderer as Unferth was. Within the constraints of that society, Beowulf epitomized conformity to the heroic code. The indictment that the poet is handing down here is not against Beowulf as an individual. As an individual, he was noble indeed, and no murderer. But the society that he represented (*and* Grendel, *and* the dragon) was a murderous society. And it is that culture that receives the indictment. For example, Beowulf as an individual does not grasp at the throne, even when Hygd offers it to him. He is not in this for himself. Nevertheless, the reason she was offering it to him in the first place was that her husband had gone off on an ill-advised smash and grab run to Friesland, *and Beowulf had gone with him* (2356–2361). Of course, it was his duty to do so, and that was the dilemma. He is a good man trapped in an evil system, and it is a system from which he cannot extricate himself.

The problem is that this warrior society, for all its emphasis on honor and fealty, had created a culture which necessarily established treachery at the heart of it. This is the meaning of both Grendel and Grendel's mother.

Grendel is treachery embodied, and Grendel's mother is the mother of that treachery, the mother of all treachery. This point is made over and over, and in numerous ways.

First, Grendel is descended from Cain, the first fratricide. Cain is therefore the father of Grendel, and, in turn, in a very real sense Grendel as kinslayer is the father of this whole society. Grendel is both outside and inside the mead-hall. He doesn't belong there (and he is not there by day) and he cannot touch the throne there, but at night he has the run of the place (167–170). In this respect, as a twisted "human," Grendel is *not* like the dragon at the end of the poem—which is more of a force of nature to be reckoned with, like an earthquake. And yet, the dragon clearly represents something about this society as well, as we shall see.

As a descendent of Cain, Grendel is also descended from Adam and Eve. He knows he belongs to the human race, and yet his bitter hatred and envy eat at him like a canker. He belongs in, and yet cannot be in. This can only mean that when he comes in (which he *has* to do, being one of them), he comes in to destroy.

Grendel corresponds in many ways to the society that he hates. He is a fratricide, and kin-slaying in that ancient world, whether we are talking about kin by blood or kin by law, is tragically common. We see this in how Unferth is welcome at Hrothgar's court even though he took the blood of his own relatives (588–590). We see this in the Lay of Finn, where Hildeburh lost both brother and son, who were on opposing sides of a blood feud (1117–1120). We see it in Beowulf's prediction of what will happen to the attempt at peace-weaving with Freawaru (2059–2064). We see it in how Beowulf and his father came to Heorot when Beowulf was a boy—Hrothgar paid the *wergild* so that Ecgtheow would not be held responsible for one of his slayings (472). We see it in Wealhtheow's concern that her sons will be killed by their cousin Hrothulf (1182–1185), just as one of them actually was. So Grendel is descended from a man who took the life of his brother. So? How does this set him apart? Who cares about *that* around these parts?

Another connection can be seen in the parity between Beowulf and Grendel. In his first raid on Heorot, Grendel snatches thirty men (122). When Beowulf comes against Grendel, he does so with the grip of thirty men (381–382). When Beowulf returns from the fight with the Frisians, he brings back thirty suits of armor (2363). Beowulf really does fight Grendel, but when he does so, it is represented to us as a civil war, *a contest between peers*. Further, it is portrayed for us as a civil war that Beowulf cannot ultimately win.

While there is no way I would want to be mistaken for a Freudian, I think there is something here that must be reckoned with. To see Beowulf and Grendel as engaged in internecine strife does not obligate us to take it in an individualistic way. We may make this point and yet escape the Freudian depths of the murky subconscious if we take it as an objective cultural struggle and not a subjective individual one. Niles compares the two approaches:

> Grendel is taken to be Beowulf's shadow self. The physical combat between these two fearsome opponents is taken to represent an inner struggle between two opposed psychic principles, one of which is associated with our moral being, the other with those dark impulses that civilized people normally suppress (Freud's ego or superego and id, respectively, whether or not these terms are invoked). To approach *Beowulf* in this manner is to read its action as a psychomachia whereby fearsome antisocial impulses threaten to overwhelm consciousness but are ultimately overcome and integrated into an expanded self. Foley (1977) takes this argument and converts it to communal history: the integration in question was a cultural one for the Anglo-Saxons as a people.[14]

---

14. John D. Niles in "Myth and History" as found in *A Beowulf Handbook* (Lincoln, NE: University of Nebraska Press, 1997), 223.

For my money, Foley takes it running away. This is a broad cultural issue, and Grendel is as much a part of it as Beowulf is. But to represent this epic poem as a portrayal of the internal subjective struggles of a narcissistic modern is as anachronistic and foolish as to start looking for Beowulf's inner child. The poet is addressing a problem which this people as a people knew they had. A poem like this should not be used as a blank screen on which we may project problems that we know *we* have. Maybe Hrothgar was actually worried about global warming or high cholesterol.

Still another link is seen in the fact that Hrothgar pays the *wergild* for the Geat warrior that Grendel ate (1055–1056). Why would he be responsible to do that unless in some sense the Danes were responsible for the death? And how could they be responsible without being identified in some way with Grendel? He was a monster all right, but he was *their* monster.

The symbolism of how Grendel dies is also very important. Beowulf does not kill him outright with the sword, but rather grapples with him barehanded. The end result is that Beowulf tears off Grendel's right arm, and Grendel lopes off in pain in order to die *somewhere else*. Beowulf is distressed by the fact that he did not kill Grendel there in the hall (962–963). He consequently did not have a carcass to show Hrothgar. If treachery had been slain where it actually manifested itself—in Heorot—the problem would have been symbolically solved. But this victory at Heorot provided only a respite, not a final victory. This is why the mother of treachery comes back the next night to seek her revenge—but even when she is also slain, and the head of Grendel is brought back to the hall, the implied statement is clear: All this is still insufficient. Grendel's mother is slain in her lair, the same place where Grendel died, and so treachery is *not* slain within the walls of Heorot.

In the victory party right afterwards, Wealhtheow is righteously maneuvering in order to protect her two sons from their cousin (1190–1194). She seats Beowulf between Hrethric and Hrothmund, in order that he might protect them from whom? From Grendel? Someone might object that Grendel is dead. Not really.

Another argument for the importance of these monsters as human treachery (and the impotence of the heroic code in the face of that treachery) can be seen in the chiastic structure of *Beowulf*. The fitts of *Beowulf* can be understood as forming a chiasm, a chiasm that helps us identify this as a central theme of the poem. The central fitt of the poem is the one in which Grendel's mother is pursued to her lair. While much more could be said about this aspect of the poem, the point can be illustrated by the two fitts on either side of this central point. In the first, Grendel's mother takes revenge by killing a warrior in Heorot (Fitt 19). Here we are again, killing people in the fellowship mead hall. In the next, Hrothgar despairs and talks (20). In the central fitt, Beowulf pursues the monster to her lair (21). She is pursued in this fitt, *and not killed*. In the next fitt, Beowulf fights with Grendel's mother (22), and this is the counterpart to Hrothgar's despairing talk. What is the link between the fitts? Hrothgar talks and Beowulf fights. But then the next fitt reveals even more. In this section (23), Beowulf actually kills Grendel's mother in her cave, just as in the corresponding fitt *she* had killed Aeschere in Heorot.[15] The two events should be seen as a stark contrast, but in some respects they are still comparable. The central point of this poem is emphasized by all this, however: in *this* society homes and halls are for killing in.[16]

Another significant aspect of this apologetic is that the *Beowulf* poet goes out of his way to honor and admire a class of aristocratic warriors

---

15. Further documentation on this can be found in my next essay, "Chiastic Structure in *Beowulf*." An actual *scholarly* documentation can be found in John D. Niles, "Ring Composition and the Structure of Beowulf" PMLA 94, no. 5 (Oct. 1979), 924–935. Niles does not address the issue of the fitts at all, but he shows how ring composition is integral to the poem, and the points drawn out in his article are generally consistent with the conclusions I drew.

16. The point is plain here (and other chiastic patterns in *Beowulf* reinforce it as well).

    A Grendel's mother kills Aeschere where he sleeps
      B Hrothgar despairs and talks
        C Beowulf pursues Grendel's mother
      B´ Beowulf fights with Grendel's mother
    A´ Beowulf kills Grendel's mother where she sleeps

who are, at the same time, utterly and entirely impotent, which is not what you want from your warriors. They can kill just about anything, *but they cannot kill what is destroying their people.* They cannot kill the cycle of violence and destruction, and any attempt to do so only fuels it further. The heroic code turns out to be the ultimate tar baby.

The central representative of this is Hrothgar. He was a magnificent warrior in his day (1680), and his prowess in battle was unquestioned. The poet goes out of his way to say that Hrothgar's valor cannot be challenged (1041–1044). And yet, his impotence in this regard is underlined time and again. The morning after Grendel is killed, Hrothgar receives the good news and comes out to look at the grisly arm. He comes, a great warrior king, having spent the night in a warm bed with Wealhtheow, and when he comes, he advances with a troop of maidens following him (922–926), a bevy of curvaceous thanes. And when his warriors are rejoicing over Beowulf's prowess, the poet tells us that they did not think to criticize Hrothgar. Why did he tell us this? The answer is obviously that the circumstances invited such criticism. Hrothgar did not fight as Beowulf did (or even as Beowulf did later on against the dragon when *he* was an old man). Usually kings are very prickly about such comparisons, and yet Hrothgar still honors Beowulf highly.[17]

At the same time, when Hrothgar speaks of how he built up his kingdom through his courage on the battlefield over the period of many years, no one hoots at him. They all knew it was true. He had been a great warrior indeed, and no one questions this, least of all the poet. It would not make the poet's point to have Hrothgar fail his people because he was a cowardly king who would not fight. No, he was a true warrior, and he saw about fifty years earlier than Beowulf did how useless this was. If Hrothgar had never been a fine warrior-king, then a defender of this way of life could reply to the poet that *this* was the problem—"If Hrothgar had only done his duty . . ." But he *had* done his duty. He had done everything expected of him. He established his people, and this meant that

---

17. "Saul has slain his thousands, and David his tens of thousands."

he enriched his people by warring with others and successfully robbing them.[18] When he settles down to enjoy the success of this, Grendel arrives to start devouring Danes. The hopelessness of this situation can be seen even in the smallest details of the poem. Chickering notes, "Clark argues convincingly that, throughout the poem, arms and armor symbolize the ambiguities at the heart of the heroic vision."[19]

All this relates to one other aspect of the poem. I argued earlier that the culture we are considering is pagan, but pagan just on the verge of conversion. If Hrothgar is a type of this society (and I think it is clear that he is), another way of seeing this is that paganism here is infirm through old age. Just as Hrothgar had once "done his duty" with enthusiasm, so this pagan society had once embraced the heroic code with the same kind of enthusiasm. But old age brings perspective, at least in some instances. Here we see that both Hrothgar and the culture around him have come to see that all they had attained was vanity and striving after wind.

The motive of Grendel in his treachery was envy. He wanted to be inside Heorot in order to be able to enjoy the creation song of the *scop*, and yet at the same time he hated the creation song of the *scop*. In the dragon, we find the other basic driving engine of this culture—greed. While Grendel did have stuff in his lair, it is clear that plunder was not really his motive. He would raid Heorot in order to eat people, and not to take their gold. His motives were malice, hatred, envy, and all the rest of that rancid bouquet.

But this dragon has a heart full of *greed*. He comes upon the lost treasure of a vanished people, and takes up residence there. After a long period of time, a runaway slave from the Geats finds his way into the dragon's barrow by accident. As he leaves, he does what every self-respecting

---

18. The Christian take on this kind of thing is illustrated in *The City of God*, where Augustine tells us (approvingly) the story of the pirate who was brought up before the emperor. The pirate asked why he was considered a pirate for doing to *ships* what the emperor did to *countries*. I forget what happened to the witty pirate then.
19. Chickering, *Beowulf*, 297. In other words, the tension between heroism and despair extends even into the *description* of armor and weapons. See also George Clark's original article, "Beowulf's Armor," *English Literary History* 32, no. 4 (December, 1965), 416-19.

Viking would do with someone else's stuff—he takes it. He takes just one cup, in order to pay off his master, but he takes it. This is an entire society that bases its economy on pillaging. Whatever generosity a king might display in being a ring-giver was a generosity that was fueled by raiding other tribes and taking what they had. The tribe that had first gathered this treasure had no doubt done it in just this way. Then a dragon comes and sleeps on top of that stash for years. A slave comes and takes one cup. But what does it matter that it is only one cup? He comes and he *takes*. That is what he does because that is what everyone does. And what happens next is what always happens next.

The dragon flies out in a rage—which is what every robbed tribe would also do—and he seeks his revenge. The externality of the dragon represents the fact that when another tribe sets sail to come against yours, there is no reasoning with it. This is just the way it is. Grendel represents that which would provoke a protest—Hrothulf ought not to have done what he did to Hrethric. Unferth ought not to have done what he did to his kin. It still happens, but treachery always calls forth a greater outrage. The malevolence of Grendel is hot, like malice always is. The rage of the dragon is cold, like the gold it is acquiring or defending. The dragon hates, but it is nothing personal. Grendel hates, and everything about it is personal. With the dragon, killing is a means to an end. With Grendel, killing is the end itself. The dragon is a night-flying outsider. Grendel is a cannibal. So this society is surrounded—hot enmity within and cold enmity without.

The dragon clearly represents the cold, pragmatic *quid pro quo* of an economy that was driven by the five-fingered discount. The last survivor laments the whole process, and puts the treasure in a barrow to await the coming of the dragon (2269–2272). After the dragon is killed, Wiglaf laments the whole process, just like the last survivor (and the chiastic structure, as well as Beowulf's word, shows us that Wiglaf is *also* a last survivor[20]). The Geats put the treasure in a barrow (with Beowulf) to await

---

20 Niles, "Ring Composition," 928.

the coming of the Swedes. This obviously puts the Swedes in the position of a "dragon." The churl who takes the cup does so to give it to his lord, who receives it gladly (2285–2288). This is just what every loyal thane would do, coming back from the wars, and it was no doubt something just like this that had provoked the Swedes. The fight with the dragon is even described in terms of a feud (2289).

This is where the poem brings us, in order to abandon us there. What can be done to save this people from their lost condition? By the end of the poem, it is absolutely certain that there is nothing that the people of this culture can do about their *lostness*. When they worship idols, they are depraved. When they win a great battle, they take the wealth of others. When they seek to repair the damage that this victorious pillaging caused, they will give a princess as a peace-weaver. But at the wedding reception some old guy will see the wrong sword on the wrong hip, and the young warrior wearing it will be swanking around like he *wants* to be killed. And if a great hero arrives from nowhere to lead the people, he can only lead them deeper into *these* traditions. Shield Sheafson drifted to the Danes in a boat—what could be more of a sign? And yet he was only able to establish them more firmly in the ways of blood. Beowulf came to the Geats, and he gave them a fifty-year respite. But even he could not deliver them.

Beowulf is not a Christ figure, although the temptation to read him this way is understandable. He delivers the people (temporarily). He descends into hell, just like in the Apostles' Creed. He is a noble and high-minded hero. He fights against wickedness and the forces of the devil. He sacrifices his life. His thanes all scatter except for Wiglaf, who is the apostle John. But I take all these similarities as ways of pointing to an almost-Christ, or, as I said in my title, the *unChrist*.

Alcuin notwithstanding, Beowulf appears to be saved as an individual. But this is not stated outright, although the hints are there. Beowulf tells Unferth that he is going to hell for his kin-slaying (589). This would be odd if there were no distinction between Beowulf and Unferth in the afterlife. Grendel also dies and goes to hell (854). But if Beowulf is going to follow Grendel there, then what was the point of all the fighting *here*? The poet says that when Shield Sheafson died, he (a noble lord) went *on Frean wære*, into "the keeping of the Lord" (27). And at the end of *Beowulf*, it says that Beowulf died and went to "seek the doom of the just"—*sawol secean soð-fæstra dom* (2822).[21] But although we may be fairly certain of all this, the argument for it is still oblique. The poet doesn't insult his Christian audience (or provoke them) by having Beowulf ascend into the presence of Christ and the saints, with angels singing all around. At the same time, we are invited to believe that he is *not* going to the place of torment.

Now if the *Beowulf* poet only hints that Beowulf is saved, how much less is he presenting him as a savior? The "salvation" that Beowulf brings is by no means everlasting. This means that Beowulf, the best and noblest that paganism could offer, one who would even probably be blessed somehow in the afterlife, could still not provide salvation for his people. That would have to await the arrival of another "hero," entirely unmentioned in the poem. If Hrothgar is the penultimate Viking hero, Beowulf is the ultimate Viking hero. And yet everything they do still comes to nothing, and *must* come to nothing. The true hero who is standing just off stage as the poem ends is Christ. He is the savior/hero, and everyone who first heard this poem was expecting Him, and was worked over by the poem to *long* for Him. But it cannot be emphasized too strongly that this coming Christ was a different *kind* of hero, one who conquers by dying, and not by killing.

To conclude and summarize my argument, I would say this. First, Grendel should be understood as a dark and necessary aspect of this noble and aristocratic society. So long as this warrior code of honor is the organizing principle of a culture, that culture will be haunted by Grendels somehow, someway. Secondly, the establishment of a warrior ruling caste necessarily creates an enemy of the society which the warriors are dedi-

---

21. These two translations are Chickering's.

cated to defend, but it is an enemy which they cannot defend against. The epitome of this is Hrothgar and also, in another (superior) way, Beowulf. The warriors with their code of honor cannot defend their people against the necessary ramifications of that code of honor whenever it is applied. In the immortal words of Pogo, "We have met the enemy, and he is us." Third, a society turned on itself in this way is not capable of fighting external enemies to a satisfactory conclusion—especially when the dragon represents the baser motives of that whole culture. Grendel is the problem within each tribe; the dragon is the problem of all the other tribes. And after you have considered the dilemma both inside and the outside, what else is there?

In another setting, the death of a dragon (and the recovery of mountains of gold) would be unqualified good news. But in this setting, the recovery of all the dragon's gold would have presented a very serious problem for the Geats even if Beowulf had not been killed. This external threat is removed, and yet this victory simply creates additional problems with all the surrounding tribes, all the other external threats. The dragon was a very satisfactory enemy, placed in such a way that whether he lives or dies, the future of the Geats is very grim indeed. And so even though the dragon of greed dies, so does Beowulf, and the gold is still there to beckon other dragons.

This is a people who would be quite eager to hear a preaching monk. And I cannot imagine that a king like Wiglaf would turn such a monk away.

Chiastic Structure in Beowulf
Douglas Wilson

INTRODUCTION

Some scholars have mentioned in passing that there are some chiastic elements in *Beowulf*. For example, the poem opens and closes with a funeral. Then I once heard it mentioned that nobody pays much attention to the fitts, whatever they are. This was invitation enough for me, and so I decided to examine the structure of *Beowulf* according to certain themes found within the fitts and see if it followed a chiastic structure. The answer is that I believe so. At the very least, I believe that what I have uncovered merits further study. It is quite possible we have not seen anything like this since the days of Wald the Woingas. (Since I saw his name in *Widsith*, I knew I just had to work it in somehow.)

BACKGROUND

Chesterton remarked somewhere that a courageous man ought to be willing to attack any error, no matter how old—but that there were some errors too old to be patronized.

A variant of this was Tolkien's objection to many of the critics of *Beowulf* in his day, and it appears to me that in some senses the criticism still applies. Certain critics have in many ways patronized this poem, neglecting to take it on its own terms. They have not looked at the elements of the poem *as it has come to us*. But perhaps a good starting assumption is that everything is there and in its place for a reason, and then to use that as a basis for seeking to understand it.

> I would express the whole industry in yet another allegory. A man inherited a field in which was an accumulation of old stone, part of an older hall. Of the old stone some had already been used in building the house in which he actually lived, not far

from the old house of his fathers. Of the rest he took some and built a tower. But his friends coming perceived at once (without troubling to climb the steps) that these stones had formerly belonged to a more ancient building. So they pushed the tower over, with no little labour, in order to look for hidden carvings and inscriptions, or to discover whence the man's distant forefathers had obtained the building material. Some suspecting a deposit of coal under the soil began to dig for it, and forgot even the stones. They all said, "This tower is most interesting." But they also said (after pushing it over): "What a muddle it is in!" And even the man's own descendants, who might have been expected to consider what he had been about, were heard to murmur: "He is such an odd fellow! Imagine his using these old stones just to build a nonsensical tower! Why did not he restore the old house? He had no sense of proportion." But from the top of that tower the man had been able to look out upon the sea.[22]

Poetic Architecture

One of the possibilities that I would like us to consider is that the fitts are stones, and that they provide an architectural structure that was common in the ancient world. Although frequently invisible to moderns, the chiasm was readily identifiable throughout the ancient world, and was *extremely* common in Scripture—a source that was obviously well known to the author of *Beowulf*. Consider this example from Jeremiah 2:27–28:

> In the time of their trouble they say,
> "Arise and save us!"
> But where are your gods that you made for yourself?
> Let them arise, if they can save you,
> In the time of your trouble.

But we might have trouble in a modern setting with modern examples.

> My wife is a good woman; her kindness to me is sure

---
22 Tolkien, 8–9.

and unfailing. When I am discouraged, she picks me up; whenever I slip her counsel sustains me. She really is steady in her character. Her goodness is quite remarkable.

Asked to outline this, we would probably not do it like this:
My wife is a good woman;
   her kindness to me is sure and unfailing.
      When I am discouraged, she picks me up;
         whenever I slip her counsel sustains me.
      She really is steady in her character.
   Her goodness is quite remarkable.

The problem for us here is that we impose our forms (or lack of them) on ancient texts, as in Tolkien's allegory. But in the ancient world, there were short chiasms like the above, and there were book-length chiasms. Getting used to this obviously requires a certain way of seeing.

Fitts and Starts

According to my calculations, the average number of lines per fitt (for those who like to keep up on such things) is somewhere between seventy-three and seventy-four. But some of them are as short as forty-two and some are as long as 141.

Just one other word about the numbering of these fitts. There are forty-three of them, which means we have our odd number that the chiasm requires. But because nothing in this life is simple, and because one of our *Beowulf* scribes was possibly a screw-up, the first fitt is unnumbered, and the numbering starts with the second one. But then, late in the poem, the realization comes (to the *second* scribe?) that everything is one off, and so he helps us jump over 30, putting us back on track to end on 43.

The diagram on pages 196–197 shows the overall chiastic structure of the poem. The line numbers and the length of each fitt are noted as well as the original fitt numbers (in Roman numerals) and my renumbering (in Arabic numerals).

VOL. 1: OLD ENGLISH

DIAGRAM: The Chiastic Structure of *Beowulf*

Chiasm line number — Summary of fitt content	Line numbers (line count)	Original fitt #	New fitt #
1 — Funeral of Shield	1–52 (52 lines)	—	1
2 — Hrothgar rises, Grendel stirs	53–114 (61 lines)	I	2
3 — Grendel kills thirty men, Heorot is deserted	115–190 (75 lines)	II	3
4 — Hrothgar broods, Beowulf sails and meets the coast guard	191–259 (68 lines)	III	4
5 — Beowulf answers the coast guard	260–321 (61 lines)	IV	5
6 — Beowulf and Wulfgar	322–372 (50 lines)	V	6
7 — Hrothgar and Beowulf meet, "Fate must go as it must"	373–456 (83 lines)	VI	7
8 — Hrothgar's speech and welcome	457–499 (42 lines)	VII	8
9 — Unferth and Beowulf clash	500–559 (59 lines)	VIII	9
10 — Sea creatures, Unferth silenced, vow to Wealhtheow	560–662 (102 lines)	IX	10
11 — Asleep in Heorot, Beowulf trusts God	663–710 (47 lines)	X	11
12 — Grendel is disturbed and advances	711–792 (81 lines)	XI	12
13 — Fight with Grendel	793–838 (45 lines)	XII	13
14 — Giddy retainers, story of Heremod	839–926 (87 lines)	XIII	14
15 — Hrothgar views arm, Beowulf wishes he had corpse	927–992 (65 lines)	XIV	15
16 — Heorot refurbished	993–1051 (58 lines)	XV	16
17 — Beowulf rewarded, "Lay of Finn" begins	1052–1126 (74 lines)	XVI	17
18 — Hengest plots revenge, Wealhtheow plans	1127–1193 (66 lines)	XVII	18
19 — Gifts bestowed on Beowulf	1194–1252 (58 lines)	XVIII	19
20 — Grendel's mother kills in Heorot	1253–1322 (69 lines)	XIX	20
21 — Hrothgar despairs and talks	1323–1384 (61 lines)	XX	21

SUPPLEMENTARY READING

22 (CENTER)	XXI	1385–1474 (89 lines)	Pursuit of Grendel's mother
21'	XXII	1475–1558 (83 lines)	Beowulf fights Grendel's mother
20'	XXIII	1559–1652 (93 lines)	Beowulf kills Grendel's mother in her lair
19'	XXIV	1653–1741 (88 lines)	Beowulf recounts story, hilt
18'	XXV	1742–1818 (76 lines)	Hrothgar admonishes and retires
17'	XXVI	1819–1889 (70 lines)	Beowulf's farewell, gifts referred to
16'	XXVII	1890–1964 (74 lines)	Beowulf sails, bad queen, Geatland refurbished
15'	XXVIII	1965–2042 (77 lines)	Hygelac receives Beowulf, Freawaru warning
14'	XXIX	2043–2145 (102 lines)	Story of Ingeld
13'	XXX	2146–2222 (76 lines)	Beowulf loyal to Hygelac, becomes king of Geats
12'	XXXI	2223–2313 (90 lines)	Dragon is disturbed and advances
11'	XXXII	2314–2392 (78 lines)	Dragon attacks, Beowulf believes he offended God
10'	XXXIII	2393–2461 (68 lines)	Beowulf hunts dragon in sorrow and despair
9'	XXXIV	2462–2603 (141 lines)	Beowulf reminisces, challenges dragon, thanes flee
8'	XXXV	2604–2695 (91 lines)	Wiglaf's speech, rally, Beowulf wounded
7'	XXXVI	2696–2753 (57 lines)	Wiglaf and Beowulf kill the dragon, see the gold
6'	XXXVII	2754–2822 (68 lines)	Beowulf sees the treasure, orders his burial
5'	XXXVIII	2823–2893 (70 lines)	Wiglaf rebukes the cowardly thanes
4'	XXXIX	2894–2947 (53 lines)	Wiglaf expects trouble, and broods
3'	XL	2948–3060 (112 lines)	Hygelac kills Ongentheow, the Swedes will be back
2'	XLI	3061–3139 (78 lines)	Cursed treasure examined
1'	XLII	3140–3185 (45 lines)	Funeral of Beowulf, no hope

Parallels Teased Out

It needs to be acknowledged at the outset that I am stating various themes within the fitts while looking for patterns or contrasts, and I am looking for things that are centered around the grand themes that have been manifest in the poem—honor, treachery, the hopelessness of this freebooting manner of life, etc. I have put in bold those pairs that I think are particularly strong, and have phrased everything accordingly. I have put in italics those I think are moderately strong. I have wanted to guard against "projecting," because I know it is quite possible to be a little too creative here. And besides, maybe God puts chiasms everywhere—Atlantic coast, Appalachians, Great Plains, Rockies, Pacific coast. Maybe chiasms are like driveway gravel, I don't know.

1 **Funeral of Shield**
1′ **Funeral of Beowulf**

2 *Trouble from Grendel looms*
2′ *Trouble from cursed treasure looms*

3 *Grendel kills thirty men, Heorot is deserted*
3′ *Hygelac kills Ongentheow, Geatland will be deserted*

4 **Hrothgar broods**
4′ **Wiglaf broods**

5 **The coast guard speaks of the difference between words and deeds**
5′ **Wiglaf speaks of the difference between words and deeds**

6 *Beowulf arrives and is introduced by name*
6′ *Beowulf departs in death*

7 *Hrothgar and Beowulf meet, "Fate must go as it must"*
7′ *Wiglaf and Beowulf kill the dragon, and see the gold*

8 *Hrothgar's speech and Beowulf welcomed*
8′ *Wiglaf's speech and Beowulf wounded*

9 **Beowulf reminisces**
9′ **Beowulf reminisces**

10 *Vow to Wealhtheow*
10′ *Beowulf hunts dragon in sorrow and despair*

11 **Beowulf trusts God**
11′ **Beowulf believes he offended God**

12 **Grendel is disturbed and advances**
12′ **Dragon is disturbed and advances**

13 *Beowulf fights with Grendel*
13′ *Beowulf does not fight with Hygelac*

14 **Story of Heremod**
14′ **Story of Ingeld**

15 *Beowulf has bad feeling about not having corpse*
15′ *Beowulf has bad feeling about Freawaru*

16 **Heorot refurbished**
16′ **Geatland refurbished**

17 **Beowulf receives gifts**
17′ **Beowulf prepares to leave with gifts**

18 *Wealhtheow plans*
18′ *Hrothgar admonishes*

19 *Beowulf keeps gifts*
19′ *Beowulf keeps hilt*

20 **Grendel's mother kills in Heorot**
20′ **Beowulf kills Grendel's mother in her lair**

21 **Hrothgar talks**
21′ **Beowulf fights**

22 (center) Pursuit of Grendel's mother

One of the things I would want to urge modern students of this classic to consider is the aesthetic value of structure and rhythm. Aspects of these values are sadly neglected in our day, almost to the point where they are entirely invisible to us. Chiasm, when it is used well, is not hidden the way a code is hidden, or a message in invisible ink. Rather, a chiasm is hidden the way a skeleton is hidden—but without that framework holding everything up, the words on the surface of the text would not have nearly the force that they do. *Beowulf* is a powerful poem, and the chiastic structure is a good part of the reason.

ANSWER KEY

Reading 2

1. Shield was essentially a marauding pirate. He ran around kicking over people's mead benches. But he is described as "one good king." As I've mentioned...be sure to take note of this as it's going to be repeated later.

2. A king gives treasure (rings) to his warriors, and they in return promise their allegiance. Treasure is meant to be given. It buys loyalty—it buys bravery. It unites.

3. Dragons (in all the old stories, not just Tolkien) plunder and kill for the sake of the treasure itself, and they "never enjoy a brass ring of it." They hoard it. For a good king, treasure is meant to be given. For a dragon, treasure is meant to be taken. For a good king, treasure unites him to his men. For a dragon, it isolates him. He kills everyone until he is left completely alone with the treasure that he can't enjoy.

4. Ring-giving happens around the table. There is table fellowship, there is generosity. The king doles out rings and in return, the thanes swear their loyalty to the ring-giver. This is the center of their culture, and the glue which holds it together.

5. The doom that eventually will destroy Heorot is burning. We are told that the problem will come from within—killing among in-laws. Remember that for the Saxons, kin-killing was almost the ultimate sin. It turned their universe upside down when someone fought against those they were supposed

to stand with. And yet, keep track of how often it happens…

6. Grendel is upset by the noise of the banquet. He hates the sound of fellowhip, and in particular, the song of the poet.

7. Grendel hears them singing about creation. Remember that this is another important insight into the Anglo-Saxon culture. Different cultures identify with different aspects of the Christian story. For the Saxons, they focused heavily on God as Creator. The Saxon word for poet is *scop*, pronounced "shope" from which we get the English word "shape." A poet is one who "shapes" and creates with his words. Given this understanding of the poet's role, God is obviously the ultimate scope—the ultimate poet. He shaped all of creation, and he does so through the power of his Word. For the Saxons, the poet is acting in imitation of God when he "shapes" with his words. Grendel hates hearing the lesser scops singing about the shaping of the world by the Great Scop.

8. Grendel was descended from Cain, and he killed his brother. Here we see that Grendel is part of the clan marked by kin-killing. Cain was the first and the archetypal kin-killer. The poet tells us that kin-killing is what will eventually be the destruction of Heorot; it seems to be the perpetual threat. Grendel, of kin-killing stock, is the current threat to the mead-hall . . . but he's the kin-killer from without. Even when he is gotten out of the way, the future threat to the fellowship of the hall is kin-killing from within.

9. Strangely enough, even though Shield is described as "a good king" he is called "the scourge of many tribes, and a wrecker of mead benches." This is exactly what Grendel is doing a mere eighty lines later.

10. When times are good, the Shieldings seem to be worshipping the Creator God. But when affliction comes, they turn back to their old gods. It says that in their hearts they "remembered Hell." This indicates a turning back, from which we can infer that they perhaps knew better and are reverting to their old ways. The poet himself adds an editorial note that this was a terrible idea, and states that the High King of Heaven was unknown to them. This leaves the exact state of things a bit ambiguous, although it is clear what the poet thinks.

11. We are told that Beowulf is the mightiest warrior of the Geats, that he's battle tested, and that his bravery, nobility, and general awesomeness is obvious to anyone who sees him.

12. This is a very open-ended question, and it will be asked every day. Look for little things—details that Tolkien borrowed and wove into his story. There are no hard and fast answers. You will likely notice things that aren't listed in the answer key at all, and that's great. A few will be listed here to help get you thinking along the right lines, but you should be looking for your own. In this section, Bilbo listens to the song and "as they sang the hobbit felt the love of beautiful things made by hands and by cunning and by magic moving through him, a fierce and a jealous love, the desire of the hearts of the dwarves." This dwarvish love of treasure and armor and gold is very Saxon. Compare this section of *Beowulf*, "Amidships the mast, they remembered and placed treasures and tackle and trust most of all, battle gear, blades edged, and bright gold and silver," with this section of the dwarves' song, "For ancient king and elvish lord, There many a gleaming golden hoard, They shaped and wrought, and light they caught, to hide in gems on hilt of sword." There is a very similar delight

in the beauty of the gold and craftsmanship of the weapons. This will continue throughout both of the books. As an aside, most of the dwarves' names are taken straight across from names of dwarves in Norse mythology, although none of them appear in *Beowulf*.

Reading 3

1. The poet focuses on the sounds of the men advancing and the way the light catches their armor. Think of our own poetic devices when we want to communicate to an audience that our hero looks really, really good or really, really intimidating. We all know that scene in the movie—it cuts to slow motion with a soundtrack that emphasizes the unspeakable coolness of the person we're watching. We watch them toss their head in slow motion, the wind catches their hair, they slowly put on the sunglasses, and they cock the gun. This is the Saxon version of that. The poet mentions the following things: the men are in marching formation, the mail shirts glint, there's a high gloss on the iron, their armor rang, the weapons clatter as as they drop them and throw themselves down on the bench.

2. Bee-Wolf is the word for "bear." Bears eat honey—thus, Bee-Wolf. (Note: There are other theories as to the meaning of the name—including "woodpecker"—but in my humble opinion this one makes the most sense.)

3. Beowulf has fought human enemies (avenging the Geats) but in this story he seems to really specialize in monsters. Here we learn of five beasts, a nest of trolls, and sea-brutes. Later we'll hear the more specific story of the sea brutes, and of course in the book itself we'll watch him kill three monsters.

4. Beowulf is going to fight without weapons, hand-to-hand. This is to bring fame and glory to his ring-giver (Hygelac) and also to gladden his heart.

5. In 442, the outcome of the battle will be deemed a judgment from God. But in 456 Beowulf says, "Wyrd goes as it must." The word for fate is "Wyrd" from which we get our modern word "weird." In Scandinavian mythology, fate was determined by Norns, or Wyrd Sisters, who wove the destinies of mankind into a tapestry that could not be changed. (Very similar to the Fates in classical mythology.) The Saxons had a heavily fatalistic mentality, and much of the residue of this survived even after the arrival of Christianity.

6. We find out that back in the day, Beowulf's father killed a man (Heatholaf) and had to go on the run. He stayed with Hrothgar early on in Hrothgar's reign, and Hrothgar helped him out by first giving him shelter, and then finally by paying the Wergild. "Were" means "man"—and "Gild" means "gold". Thus, the wergild is the man-gold, or restitution money paid to the clan if you had killed one of them. This was another way of seeking to avert an out-and-out blood feud.

7. Unferth is motivated by envy. He's clearly bothered by Beowulf showing up and being so much admired. It's obviously embarrassing to a thane to have outside help show up in order to take care of a problem. After all, whose primary responsibility should Grendel be? Hrothgar has been the ring-giver, so now is the moment that his thanes should be giving their lives to fight for him. Beowulf showing up makes Unferth look pretty bad. (Especially when he says things about fighting Grendel without weapons.) Given the

bond between a ring-giver and his thanes, either Grendel or Unferth should be dead right now. The fact that they are both alive is a testimony to Unferth's cowardice. As long as he could tell himself that Grendel was an impossible foe then he could feel good about himself. Beowulf's arrival made that excuse seem a bit weak, and so he does his best to discredit Beowulf.

8. Again, if you're finding different things than those listed here, that's great. One interesting point is hearing in line 422 that Beowulf had taken out a troll's nest. Of course we've just seen the dwarves and Bilbo stumble across a trolls' nest, but we can be fairly certain that Beowulf's trolls weren't named Tom, Bert, and William.

Reading 4

1. The contest had to occur on the Baltic Sea side of Geatland. The very closest shore of Finland is twenty miles east of point C:VI on the map (pg. 12). Assuming that he didn't start in Sweden (which was generally hostile territory) but rather down in Geatland, this makes the trip quite a bit longer.

2. Unferth is a kin-killer. As already discussed, kin-killing was seen as the ultimate sin. Kin-killing is what got Cain banished, and Grendel is the embodiment of that sin. Unferth is therefore clearly marked as being the wrong kind of guy.

3. One of them should be dead. The only explanation for this state of things is cowardice on the part of Unferth.

4. We are obviously supposed to pity Hrothgar. He's been plagued by this horrible monster for years, and has had to desert his

magnificent hall. He's also old. But at the same time, later in the book we'll see how Beowulf handles a similar situation—an old king with a monster attacking his kingdom. Beowulf's response is quite a bit different from Hrothgar's. While the poet is sympathetic with Hrothgar, it does seem obvious that we're meant to notice the contrast—and we should take note of the fact that Hrothgar went off to bed, leaving the defense of his hall to a foreigner. In the same way that we wonder why both Grendel and Unferth are still alive . . . we also wonder why Grendel and Hrothgar are both still alive.

5. Obviously, in *Beowulf* we have an evil, nasty creature sneaking in from the marshes, and in Tolkien we see some evil, nasty creatures appearing out of the tunnels and caves of a mountain. We also see the goblins outraged at the sight of the ancient sword the dwarves had pulled from the trolls' lair. Keep that in mind as you get further into Beowulf. The concept of ancient and recognizable swords is a theme that will show up repeatedly.

Reading 5

1. Because Grendel uses no weapons, Beowulf has renounced all weapons as well, in order to bring more glory to Hygelac. His men did not, and they attempted to help in the fight. We then find out that Grendel is protected against all weapons, which is presumably why no one has been able to kill him thus far. Beowulf was fighting bare-handed out of a sense of nobility, and that turned out to be the key to killing the monster. This is also the beginning of an interesting theme throughout the poem—Beowulf's unusual relationship to his weapons.

2. The first time we heard the phrase, "what a good king that was," it was about Shield. He was a good king because of his amazing skills at wrecking mead-halls and kicking over the benches. Almost immediately after this we are introduced to Grendel, who wrecks mead-halls and kicks over the benches, and he is clearly the villain of the piece. Either the poet noticed this seeming contradiction or he didn't. If he didn't, then it remains a simple contradiction. If he did notice this, then he's making a deliberate point that we, as the audience, are supposed to pick up on. And if this is the case, then when he says, "what a good king that was," we are supposed to feel some irony. He then uses the identical phrase about Hrothgar. We are told that he left his mead-hall to be defended from the monster by a foreigner, and he went back to the queen's palace with her. In the morning, he shows back up with all the women to hear the results of the fight. We are told that no one blamed him, which of course makes us realize that it's understandeable that someone might blame him. The poet then says, "what a good king that was." It appears that the same irony is present in the phrase this time as was there the first time it was used. Both Shield and Hrothgar are good kings, but . . . . The poet leaves that part unspoken.

3. "Powerful kinsmen came together, close in friendship. Heorot was full of friends; at least for present. Betrayal and treachery had not yet been tried." This tells us again that although Heorot has been saved from the kin-killing monster who attacks from without, it will eventually be destroyed through the treacherous kin-killing that will manifest itself inside the hall.

4. Hopefully you have noticed some things on your own that

Tolkien has been pulling from *Beowulf*. In this section in particular, he is drawing on the Saxon love of riddles. Another example of their fascination with riddles is *The Book of Exeter*, a tenth century volume that has a collection of over ninety riddles. Tolkien is clearly drawing from that in this chapter of *The Hobbit*.

Reading 6

1. The center of this story is clearly Hildeburh. The story opens with her grief as she watches the burning of her brother and son. The story closes with her husband being treacherously murdered by her brother's people. She is carried home, having lost everything. As the readers, we are supposed to focus on the tragedy of the feud that leaves this woman desolate. There is something very interesting about the poet's decision to tell the story this way. There is another Anglo-Saxon account of the same battle which is recorded separately in what is known as "The Finnsburg Fragment." The essentials of the story are the same, with one very notable difference. In the Finnsburg Fragment there is no mention of Hildeburh at all. The battle is presented simply as any other glorious battle. For some reason, though, our poet here wants us to focus on this blood-feud and see it from the perspective of the woman who lost absolutely everything. So rather than seeing this blood-feud as noble and glorious, we're supposed to see it as a tragedy.

2. Immediately after the Finnsburg Episode, the poet brings in Wealhtheow, another peace-weaver. We just heard how badly things went for Hildeburh, and then we turn our attention to Wealhtheow who is talking about how well her family is going to get along after Hrothgar dies. We already know

that Heorot will be destroyed by treachery, and the poet underscores this point by placing Unferth the notorious kin-killer in the center of the family group.

3. We've seen that in some way, blood-feuds and kin-killing are opposites. In a blood-feud, relatives are avenging one another, which is what makes kin-killing so monstrous; it's an inversion of the natural order of things. So these two things would seem to be opposites. Grendel is obviously the embodiment of kin-killing, since he is descended from Cain. His mother comes to avenge him, and so she is the embodiment of vengeance. But rather than being enemies and opposites, they are mother and son, and both are monsters. The poet is doing something very profound here, but very understated. He makes it obvious, but doesn't come right out and say what he means, which leaves us wondering if he did it on purpose or not. Is he trying to show us that the Saxon idea of vengeance is wrong?

4. In both *Beowulf* and in *The Hobbit*, we see in this section that getting rid of one monster problem only reveals that the creatures had allies. Beowulf rids the hall of one plague, only to discover a new one in Grendel's mother. In *The Hobbit*, they have escaped the goblins only to be pinned down by the evil wolves. In both books, there is a whole world of evil creatures, in marshes, in mountains, in oceans, in forests. Killing one can sometimes just make things worse.

READING 7

1. Beowulf tells Hrothgar that it is better to avenge your friends than to sorrow in silence. But the poet has just finished showing us the tragic effects of vengeance. In the Finnsburg

Episode, we seem to be intended to see the futility of being motivated by a desire for revenge, but here Beowulf seems to be advocating revenge as a way of winning fame before death, and in this case it seems very noble and we readers are supposed to be sympathetic. One explanation would be that the poet feels that when it comes to monsters, revenge is completely vindicated in a way that it isn't amongst humans. Another explanation would be that the poet is showing us that it's futile, but noble. Or, he may be showing us that even though there are noble heroes like Beowulf in this life, the whole thing is dominated by tragedy and futility.

2. Before Beowulf descends into the lake, he asks Hrothgar to watch out for his men. Imagine for a moment a culture that operates with ring-givers and thanes. If a ring-giver dies and his men are still alive . . . what possible explanation can there be? They should have died for him, or with him. If they remain alive, they are tainted forever as cowards. Why would any mead-hall would welcome a thane whose ring-giver was dead? There is a Saxon poem called *The Wanderer* which gives a heart-rending description of being in that position—forever an outcast. Beowulf is taking care that his men are not left like that, and he asks Hrothgar to look out for them.

3. This is something interesting that the poet is doing—and we're unsure of what we're supposed to make of it. Neither Grendel nor his mother can be killed with regular weapons. Beowulf stumbles on that secret accidentally in Grendel's case, by deciding for completely other reasons to fight him bare-handed. Before facing Grendel's mother, however, he inexplicably decides to trade swords with Unferth, and although we know that it's a good sword, we also know

that it's a kin-killer's sword. Beowulf takes it with him, and it proves completely ineffective. He's back to fighting bare-handed again, until he discovers an ancient sword that was forged by the giants. This is a weapon that will kill Grendel's mother and can hack through Grendel's neck, but as soon as it does so it melts and leaves nothing behind but the hilt. We'll see some of these same features again in later fights, which means that the poet is doing something intentional here.

4. Beorn is a very interesting figure, and in this section, Tolkien is borrowing heavily from the Saxon world. Hopefully you noticed the mead-hall. Beorn lives in a great hall, and serves his guests mead. (Obviously the one thing lacking is companions!) Beorn's name itself is the Saxon word for bear, which of course is also what Beowulf's name means. Beorn is a skin-changer, which is also a feature of old Norse mythology. (We even get our word werewolf from a Saxon kenning "wer-wulf" which literally means "man-wolf.")

5. In *Beowulf*, it also seems that the giant sword Beowulf used may have had some kind of ability to glow after a kill. After Beowulf kills Grendel's mother, a light shines, and he inspects the cave with sword held high. (1572-1576) Remember that in Chapter 4 of *The Hobbit*, Gandalf's sword "was bright as blue flame for delight in the killing of the great lord of the cave."

Reading 8

1. In this section we hear Hrothgar reflecting on life and temptation in a way that's quite profound. He sees what kind of man Beowulf is, and he can tell that he'll be a great king

Answer Key

someday. He's offering some advice now, because he knows he'll probably never see Beowulf again, so he talks about a common temptation that comes to great men—that of pride. He gives the example of Heremod, once a mighty man, who came to a bad end through stumbling at this particular point. In describing pride, he uses the imagery of a night maurader who will come in and destroy your soul, while the sentry sleeps, in just the way Grendel has terrorized Heorot. Grendel's attacks had left the mead-hall desolate and abandoned, in just the same way that the attack of pride caused Heremod to end his days desolate and abandoned. We also learn that after becoming proud, Heremod got greedy and refused to give rings. He turned on his own men and hoarded his treasure. This is what a dragon does—devours and hoards. A ring-giver is supposed to give generously in order to ensure loyalty, a dragon kills in order to take the treasure and sit on it. As Hrothgar is giving Beowulf advice, he is warning him to not become a dragon king.

2. Hopefully you're still noticing things on your own. In this section, we see the dwarves and the hobbit going into Mirkwood—a dark and nasty forest filled with dark and nasty creatures. It's against everyone's better judgement to go in there. In a lot of ways, tracking Grendel's mother to the Lake of Monsters is similar. Everyone knows to stay away from that place, even the animals. It's deep in the bogs and crags and fens, populated by monstrous beasts.

Reading 9

1. The poet has already given us one tragic story of a peace-weaver in the Finnsburg Episode in which we are led to infer

that peace-weaving isn't always effective. Here the poet more explicit. He just goes ahead and has Beowulf telling Hygelac how it's probably all going to go terribly wrong. The poet seems to feel that attempting to stop a blood-feud is a near impossibility, and that vengeance is a monster that can never be satisfied.

2. Beowulf has made his way back to his own land and his ring-giver Hygelac. If you look at the family tree at the beginning of this book, you'll see that Beowulf is Hygelac's nephew. Not just any nephew—he's the son of Hygelac's sister. In Saxon culture, that relationship was a very strong one. Their kenning for this was sister-son, and the bond you had to your sister-son was very tight. Tolkien works this in as well, when Thorin announces himself to the guards of Laketown, he introduces Fili and Kili as "the sons of my father's daughter." This tells us that Fili and Kili were the sister-sons of Thorin, just as Beowulf was the sister-son of Hygelac. The sons of your brother were still kin, but it was not as close of a relationship as the sons of your sister.

Reading 10

1. Beowulf has been king for fifty years when the dragon shows up, which is the exact amount of time that Hrothgar had been king when Grendel first showed up. The poet clearly wants us to see this, and it sheds some light on Hrothgar. We were sympathetic with him for not fighting Grendel himself—after all, he's old. But we see a very different reaction from Beowulf when he's in a similar situation. This should, obliquely, make us realize that even though we were told that no one thought to blame Hrothgar . . . blaming Hrothgar is almost inevitable.

2. We know that turning on your own people is the kin-killing sin of Cain, of Unferth, and of Heremod. Beowulf is so far away from this sin that even when he's offered the throne he refuses to take it until everyone with a rightful claim on it is dead. He is loyal to Hygelac not just during his life—he is loyal to his family after his death. Hrothgar had warned Beowulf against the pride that leads to treachery, and we see here that Beowulf stays away from that all his life.

3. Both of the previous times we've heard this, there has been a possible irony in the statement. (See Day 5, Question 2) In this case, we are told that Beowulf is a good king immediately after we hear that he's suiting up to go fight the dragon. In Hrothgar's case we heard this phrase immediately after we see him coming back with the women in the morning after not fighting Grendel. In Shield's case we are told he was a good king immediately after we learn about his ransacking and pillaging ways as he destroyed mead-halls. In Beowulf's case we are told this immediately after we learn that he shows deference and loyalty, and is faithful to all the vows he made to his ring-giver in the mead-hall. It seems that Beowulf is being held up for us as a contrast to earlier "good kings"— both of whom really were good kings in the Saxon estimation. But with the other two there was a tang of hypocrisy—with Beowulf we seem to have been given a picture of a truly "good king."

4. Of course in this section we some serious plot parallels. The dragon in *Beowulf* is wakened after a long sleep when a thief comes in and steals a single cup. When the dragon wakes he misses the cup, and in his rage he goes out and terrorizes the kingdom. Tolkien borrowed those details straight across.

Bilbo is the designated burglar for the expedition, and so he sneaks in while the dragon sleeps and takes a single cup. The dragon wakes and notices the absence, and this is what sets him off after being asleep for so long that some of the Lake men had stopped believing in the dragon at all.

Reading 11

1. There are some interesting parallels between Christ and Beowulf in this section. One obvious one is that Beowulf is fighting a serpent. He goes in alone on behalf of his people. He has a band of twelve. They desert him and run. We'll see more parallels in the next section as well.

2. Smaug is destroying Laketown, and this is much like the devastation of the dragon in *Beowulf*. We also see Beowulf's sword being unable to pierce the dragon and the arrows from the Lake men simply bouncing off. Of course in Tolkien, Bard has been given the secret information about the one vulnerable spot on Smaug's belly—Beowulf doesn't have that advantage.

Reading 12

1. As we've seen throughout the book, treasure is meant to be used to secure valor. A ring-giver is generous so that when he needs the loyalty of his men, he will have it. Heremod was the dragon king who hoarded his wealth, a good king gives it away. But that generosity will come back to him when he needs faithful warriors. On the other hand, how does a ring-

giver acquire the treasure that he gives? Obviously, through valour. A good king would have been a loyal thane once, and he would have given his valor and received treasure from his own ring-giver. After he is a king, he would acquire more treasure through conquering other kingdoms (valor). Or, in Beowulf's case, he would use his valor to win back ancient treasures from the clutches of monsters. Either way, both valor and gold are meant to be given away, and when they are, both bring in a rich harvest. In other words, the Saxons traded iron for gold and gold for iron.

2. We'll see this more specifically mentioned in the next section, but Beowulf has managed to avenge himself. He doesn't need an avenger. Throughout the poem we've seen the endless need for vengeance, and how it's never satisfied until everyone is dead. Here, Beowulf gives a last gift to his people by killing his own killer. No one else needs to die to pay for the death of Beowulf.

3. Wiglaf obviously has no sympathy for these men. He points out to them that they were handchosen by Beowulf because he thought they were his most loyal men. He had given their armor and their weapons to them, and it was effort he had just thrown away. He tells them they will be outcasts, they and their families will be exiled, their lands will be seized, and no mead-halls will ever take them in again.

4. In this section, Thorin is becoming what Hrothgar warned Beowulf about. Remember how the example of Heremod keeps coming up in *Beowulf*. The temptation of a king to turn into a dragon is a common one, and one that Thorin is falling into. Rather than using treasure to cement loyalty, he

is hoarding treasure in a way that creates enemies.

READING 13

1. Beowulf ends his life avenging himself. None of his people have to die to pay for his death. Beowulf spent his life keeping peace, and even in death he secured peace for his people, as far as the dragon was concerned. However, old blood feuds are still alive—feuds that began well before Beowulf's time. He managed to keep them inactive, but he couldn't erase them. His death leaves his people vulnerable, and all their enemies will seize that opportunity. This means that all the Christ figure symbolism is very limited in its scope. Beowulf could save his people from a dragon, but he couldn't defeat all of their enemies. Although there is a great deal of Christological symbolism, the obvious point of difference is that there is no resurrection for Beowulf. The poem ends just like Beowulf, in flames. But why would the poet do that? If he is a Christian poet, why end in despair? Why make Beowulf an obvious Christ figure, and then cut out the most important part of the crucifixion story? If you're interested in thinking through this question more, you can read the previous essay by Douglas Wilson: *Beowulf: The Un-Christ*.

2. In this last section there are a few similarities between *Beowulf* and *The Hobbit*. In both, there was the burial of a king. Beowulf was heaped in treasure, Thorin had the arkenstone laid on his breast and the elven sword placed on his tomb. Dain became king under the mountain, and we are told that the other dwarves remained with Dain, "for Dain dealt his treasure well." This of course sounds like the Saxon ring-giving. When Bilbo makes his way back to Beorn's hall, we

are told that men came from far and wide to feast. Beorn became a great chieftain, which means that the mead-hall finally had the companionship which was so notably missing last time they were there. Also, when they found themselves back at Rivendell, the description of the feast and the songs and the "tales, and yet more tales, tales of long ago, and tales of new things, and tales of no time at all" sounds very much like the scop singing in the Saxon mead-hall, telling tales of Siegmund and dragons and giants and Hengest and Finn. Lastly, we are told of the unfortunate end of the old Master of Laketown. "Being of the kind that easily catch such disease he fell under the dragon-sickness, and took most of the gold and fled with it, and died of starvation in the Waste, deserted by his companions." He might have been named Heremod, but we can't be sure.

Made in the USA
Middletown, DE
10 September 2024

60752937R00132